CARL ORFF

Carl Orff

(Photographed by Atelier Fayer, Vienna, February, 1955)

CARL ORFF

ANDREAS LIESS

Translated by
Adelheid and Herbert Parkin

CALDER AND BOYARS
LONDON

FIRST PUBLISHED IN GREAT BRITAIN IN 1966
BY CALDER AND BOYARS LIMITED
18 BREWER STREET - LONDON, W.1
ALL RIGHTS RESERVED
© ATLANTIS VERLAG, ZÜRICH, 1955
© THIS TRANSLATION CALDER AND BOYARS LTD. 1966

SET IN MONOTYPE 12 ON 14 PT. BEMBO AND
PRINTED IN THE REPUBLIC OF IRELAND BY
HELY THOM LIMITED, DUBLIN

CONTENTS

31298

ILLUSTRATIONS

FOREWORD
TO THE ENGLISH EDITION

Anyone wishing to write about Orff must be aware of the chief significance of his work. Otherwise it would be pointless to put pen to paper. The undertaking involves exploring to the very roots of the theatre—its basic mimetic material and world symbolism. He must penetrate to the most elementary and the most sublime; pure play and pure spirit. One cannot do justice to Orff's creative work by considering only its musical aspects. Alongside his musical primitivism, one must place the stimulating force of his ideas on the art of dramatic presentation; an art which, in a resonant, vibrant room, makes the singing and playing of vibrant people an allegory of life.

K. H. RUPPEL

PRELUDE

Aт the Salzburg Festival of 1949 I heard *Antigonae* for the first time, and it made a lasting impression on me. I also met Carl Orff. During the following years my interest in Orff developed as I heard more of his music. I asked Orff if he would agree to my writing a book about him, and he consented. Subsequently I enjoyed, on many occasions, the hospitality of his home in Munich, spending there weeks of study and conversation. He produced the scores of works long laid by. And he talked. Orff is a delightful raconteur.

He imposed on me the strict condition that my book should be concerned exclusively with his music; all those biographical details in which psychologists or a sensation-hungry public might be interested, were to be excluded. Occasionally Orff would offer a remark which seemed to me to illumine some aspect of his character; but he would immediately insert an ironic qualification. Partly consciously and partly sub-consciously he discourages any close approach. 'A life story cannot be written,' he says, 'until the life is completed. Anything else is deceit and self-deception.' He will, however, discuss the strata and cross-currents of his life; you can get no idea of Orff otherwise. What he wishes to be known of his vocation and his early work is collected in this Prelude.

Carl Orff comes from a Bavarian family of army officers. He was born in Munich in July 1895, the same year as Hindemith. After studying at the Gymnasium, he spent several years from 1913 at the Akademie der Tonkunst. From his fifth year he had private tuition in piano, organ and 'cello. His great ambition while at school, to study the kettle-drum, was not realised. Later, his principal teachers were Beer-Walbrunn and Hermann Zilcher. Both were great teachers, but Orff did not find them sympathetic to his approach to music. Orff, indeed, should be considered self-taught. His first songs were published before he had had his first lesson in harmony. He acquired his basic knowledge from the study of the works of the old masters.

Orff was a good pupil at the Gymnasium and had an imaginative bent. His favourite subjects were German Essay, Literature, Latin, Greek, Botany, and Natural Science. He collected insects and was an enthusiastic gardener.

But he was drawn so decidedly to music that there was no question of his adopting any other profession. From his childhood to the present day, he has never enjoyed piano practice. His piano technique is unremarkable, though his interpretations are invariably of great interest. It is not surprising, therefore, that he was more eager to play his own improvisations than to practise the Czerny studies.

Improvising in both words and music is, indeed, his great passion. In 1905 his first story was published in a children's magazine. At the same time, he was writing a romantic nature book. Soon afterwards he began to compose music for the puppet-plays he had written. His puppet orchestra comprised a piano, a violin, a zither, a glockenspiel—and the kitchen range, used extensively to produce the effect of thunder. He himself pounded the piano— 'very loudly,' he recalled—in this orchestra, the other members of which were his young sister and several school friends.

His first serious compositions were songs to his own texts, which an understanding mother helped him to write down. Of great importance to him was the experience of playing, with his mother, piano transcriptions of all the symphonic and operatic music within his grasp. They sang duets also, for as a child Orff had a fine treble voice. His home was rich in music; string quartets and piano quintets were played. The boy absorbed music continually, both at home and, from the age of ten, at the concert-hall and the theatre.

At the age of sixteen, Orff had his first work published. This consisted of several collections of songs issued in 1911 by Ernst Germann, Munich/Leipzig.

op. 12, Eliland, ein Sang vom Chiemsee (Karl Stieler)
op. 13, Märchen (Max Haushofer)
op. 15, Des Herzens Slüzzelin
op. 17/2, Toskanische Volkslieder (P. Heyse)
op. 18/1, Der Tod und die Liebe (Münchhausen)

All his first published works were songs. Before these publications, he had composed a great many songs and song-cycles. The power of his creative urge is demonstrated by the fact that between January and July 1911, he wrote some fifty songs to texts by Uhland, Lenau, Hölderlin, Münchhausen, Baumbach, Storm, Lingg, Heine (Die Wallfahrt nach Kevelaar), Arndt, Nietzsche and others, as well as settings of Old German poems from the Edda saga. All this he achieved with no instruction in theory.

In May 1912 he finished his first full-scale choral work: Also sprach Zarathustra, in three parts op. 14:—

1. Nachtlied, 2. Mitternacht, 3. Vor Sonnenaufgang.

The score is written in the handwriting of a child, impetuous, but with clearly defined character. The work is for baritone solo, three choirs and orchestra with organ. Each part is differently orchestrated.

1. Oboe d'amore, English horn, clarinet, bassoon, contra-bassoon, 4 horns, trombone, tuba and tam-tam.

2. Oboe, clarinet, bass clarinet, 2 bassoons, contra-bassoon, 4 horns, 3 trumpets, 2 tubas, tam-tam, timpani and harp.

3. Flutes, oboe, oboe d'amore, English horn, clarinet, bass clarinet, bassoon, contra-bassoon, brass, pianos (!), 2 harps and mixed percussion.

Not having the space here to discuss in detail the stylistic qualities of the work, one must simply point to the instrumentation as evidence of Orff's original and well-developed tonal imagination.

In July 1913 Orff completed his first opera: *Gisei, das Opfer*, Music-drama with libretto freely adapted from *Terakoya* by K. Florenz, a romantic interpretation of a traditional Japanese play. The style of this work (op. 20) shows clearly that Orff's most important influence was Debussy. Here Orff uses the conventional full orchestra for the first time.

Apart from the strings, which include violas and 'cellos, the orchestra is made up of 3 flutes, quadruple woodwind, 4 horns, 3 trumpets, 3 trombones, 2 tubas, timpani, triangle, cymbals, bass drum, tam-tam, glockenspiel, glass harmonica, piano and 2 harps. There is a stage orchestra consisting of 4 violins, 6 violas, 2 piccolos, 2 flutes, 3 bassoons, 3 trumpets, 3 trombones, 2 tubas, timpani, gong, thunder sheet, wind machine, glass harmonica and harp, with mixed choir off-stage. As tone-colour plays so large a part in Orff's work, it seems important to list the instruments as evidence of his early originality.

Op. 21, written in January 1914 is entitled, *Tanzende Faune*, a piece for orchestra. With this work his period of juvenilia comes to an abrupt end.

In 1914 Orff planned a large symphonic work with soloists and choir: *Treibhauslieder*, based on Maeterlinck. This marked the end of his Debussy period. Now, for the first time, Schoenberg, with his *Fünf Orchesterstücke* became important to him. Orff transcribed Schoenberg's first Chamber Symphony for piano duet. The *Treibhauslieder* Symphony was never completed and, apart from a few sketches, was eventually destroyed.

At this time, Orff made sketches of other operatic works based on Maeterlinck (*Aglavaine et Sélysette, La mort de Tintagile*) and Strindberg (*Dream-play*). These fragments were destroyed, as was a symphonic poem in the style of Richard Strauss, based on Maeterlinck's *Monna Vanna*. There survive from this time two string quartets, choral music, songs with orchestral accompaniment to words by Dehmel, and incidental music.

During these years, Orff broke away from the decadence of the 1890s, and turned, with full conviction, to old music.

From 1915 to 1917 he was repetiteur and conductor at the Munich Kammerspiele. This appointment was of great importance to him, and it is not fortuitous that the theatre has been to Orff a greater source of inspiration than the opera house. At this time drama was at the centre of his interests and the Kammerspiele under Falckenberg, performing plays by Strindberg, Wedekind, Brecht and others, was at its finest.

These experiences are fundamental to an account of many of the characteristics of Orff's later work. The first sketches for *A Midsummer Night's Dream* were being written at this time and the theatre continued to influence him right down to the time of *Bernauerin* and *Astutuli*. He himself conducted Zilcher's incidental music to Falckenberg's world-famous production of *As You Like It* many times.

Orff retains feelings of great gratitude and devotion to this producer of genius.

In 1917 Orff joined the army. This was a period of emotional crisis which involved a complete change in his work.

In 1918, though, he returned to the theatre (in Mannheim and Darmstadt) and came once more under the sway of Richard Strauss (*Salome*, *Elektra*), and also of Hans Pfitzner (*Palestrina*). These operas impressed Orff profoundly and he still retains the greatest admiration for them.

He wrote more music for the theatre. Büchner's *Leonce und Lena*, with music by Orff, was performed in Berlin and elsewhere. He continued to be occupied by *A Midsummer Night's Dream* and by Shakespeare in general.

In 1919 he resigned from his theatrical engagements to retire to Munich and devote himself entirely to composition. He did, however, accept some pupils. His first famous pupil was Karl Marx, who was only two years Orff's junior.

Orff became greatly interested in expressionist writing, particularly that of Franz Werfel. He wrote a large album of Franz Werfel Lieder, which may be accounted the first realisation of a true, individual style. He also set to music words by Trakl, Klabund, Nietzsche and others. The last work of this period was completed in June 1920. This was Werfel's *Des Turmes Auferstehung* for two choirs and large orchestra with organ. The orchestra consists of 6 flutes, 6 oboes, 6 bassoons, (no clarinets or horns!), 4 trumpets, 4 trombones, timpani, bell, 4 harps, 4 pianos and strings. This mammoth work is as firm in construction as it is colourful in sound. It has never been performed. Apart from some minor compositions, it marked the end of his second period.

From 1921 Orff studied for a further year with Heinrich Kaminski. After this, he turned away entirely from contemporary music and occupied himself exclusively with the old masters. Lassus, Palestrina and Gabrieli led inevitably to Monteverdi— a name of prime importance throughout Orff's life.

At the same time, the new movement in ballet, which was

centred in München-Schwabing, fascinated him. Leistikow, von Derp, Sacharoff, Sent Mahesa, Laban and, above all, the great Mary Wigman were dancers whose art and development he followed with particular interest.

It is characteristic of Orff that, apart from a four-part setting by Lassus, no music interested him so much as the accompaniment to a dance played on African rattles. After Falckenberg's theatrical art, after the Renaissance music, this was the third formative experience. Ideas for a reformation of the theatre began to crystallise. The problem of unifying music and movement was posed.

Another important event was Orff's meeting with Dorothee Günther. In 1924, he founded with her the Günther Schule, which aimed to unify the disciplines of dancing and gymnastics. Dorothee Günther herself wrote (in the *Einführung zu Grundlagen und Aufbau des Musikschulwerkes*, 1935) about her aims: 'When I founded the Günther Schule in 1924, I wanted to discover a method of reviving the natural unity of music and movement— music and dance; a method which would be available not only to a few natural artists but would solve the educational problem of awakening in everyone the sense of rhythmic movement, and of stimulating a love of dancing and music making—a general freedom of expression and receptivity. This unity of music and movement was not to be based on incidental and subjective experience but on their elemental relationship, in that they arise from a single source.'

It would take us too far afield to discuss all the problems that occupied Orff at this time. But he had at his disposal in the Günther Schule an ideal field for educational and artistic research, from which developed, up to 1930, the first great idea of the *Schulwerk*. He created a new range of percussion instruments, helped by the advice of Curt Sachs, and the practical co-operation of the great harpsichord and piano builder, Carl Maendler, who constructed the first new xylophone and other related instruments.

Gunild Keetman, Orff's pupil and eventual collaborator, who had a unique gift both for music and movement was ultimately responsible for the realisation of the *Schulwerk*. (Equally his pupil and assistant Hans Bergese was of great help in perfecting the *Schulwerk*.)

The dance group of the Günther Schule, which was disbanded in 1943 when its home was bombed, spread these new ideas during many foreign tours under the direction of Dorothee Günther and Maja Lex—as did the group of the Wigman Schule. The unity of music and movement was realised with unique force. The instruments of Orff's own percussion orchestra, to which recorders were added, were played by the dancers themselves. Gunild Keetman wrote all the music for the dances.

This dance orchestra provided valuable experience for Orff in developing his handling of the percussion in his later work. Orff was never, as a composer, bound to his study; he drew his inspiration directly from life.

Parallel to these studies, Orff's work on Renaissance music continued. His first version of Monteverdi's *Orfeo* was performed in the National Theatre of Mannheim on the 25th March, 1925. The text of this work was, like Orff's other Monteverdi realisations, written in collaboration with Dorothee Günther.

This realisation of *Orfeo* retained to a large extent the old instrumentation (cornetts, theorbos, etc.). It is of importance only as an experiment which aroused some interest and discussion.

In the autumn of 1925, the second of Orff's Monteverdi realisations, *Tanz der Spröden* (*Ballo delle Ingrate*), was performed in Karlsruhe. This version of the work was never performed elsewhere.

After the realisation of *Klage der Ariadne*, for which Orff himself wrote the text, he worked on *L'Incoronazione di Poppea* and *Il ritorno d'Ulisse in patria*. These were never completed.

A *Kleines Konzert* for wind and harpsichord, 1927, was the first work of Orff published by Schott und Söhne of Mainz. Subsequently, this house was responsible for the publication of all Orff's music. The *Kleines Konzert*, like the other music written at this time, has been withdrawn.

There remains from this period only the *Entrata*. This work for five separately placed orchestral groups is based on *The Bells* by William Byrd. The Byrd piece is built on a rocking, bell-like ostinato figure of two notes. The *Entrata* is designed as a festival overture. The widely spaced orchestras produce the effect of a resonant room. Two of the five orchestras each consist of 3 flutes, 3 oboes, harp, two pianos, glockenspiel and strings. A centrally placed main orchestra consists of organ (or trautonium), 6 horns, 4 trombones, 3 trumpets, 2 tubas, timpani, cymbals, bassoons and double basses. On both sides are raised groups each containing 4 trumpets and timpani. The music comes to a climax, but there is no development. The ceremonial character is shown only through a static, heraldic quality. K. H. Ruppel has written with particular relevance about the work in the following terms: 'Even when Orff writes absolute music, as in the *Entrata* for five orchestras, there is behind it a clearly visualised event, either a great procession or some improvised ceremonial so dear to the decorative taste of the Renaissance or the Baroque. Wherever the elemental sense of the theatre finds expression, Orff draws his inspiration.' This was written after a later performance of the work which, in its original form, was first performed in 1930 under Hermann Scherchen. A revised version was given its first performance in February 1941 under Konvitschny in Frankfurt-am-Main.

Clearly, at the end of the 1920s, Orff was putting all his energy into finding his true theatre.

In 1929 Orff's *Cantus-firmus-Sätze* was published by Schott. It is now out of print and has been withdrawn. In 1954, however, there appeared under the same title, as part of the *Jugendmusik*, a new edition of ten of the twelve 'old melodies for voice or instruments'. The old text, the faux-bourdon and other technical features point distinctly to Orff's studies at that time. Example 1 shows a typical setting (O Lux).

EXAMPLE 1

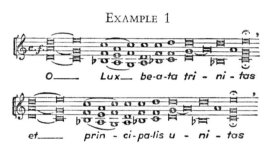

In 1929 Orff worked on a revision of the Werfel songs of 1920/1921, arranging them for chorus, 3 pianos and percussion. Here for the first time is the orchestration which was to reach its full development in *Antigonae*. Orff called the collection in which these cantatas appeared, *Das Werkbuch*. His foreword expresses the intention of the work in the following terms: '*Das Werkbuch* contains choral and instrumental settings which do not derive essentially from exercises for the concert platform. They seek to achieve a unification of spiritual attitudes, which will lead the individual from his subjective isolation to a binding and universally valid sense of community. The simplicity of the arrangements and the choice of media result from this aim. By sacrificing everything which would make the music difficult to perform, it is hoped that the highest degree of intensity may be achieved.'

Originally, five volumes were planned. From these appeared in 1930, as *Werkbuch I*, the following cantatas to texts by Franz Werfel:

I. *Veni creator spiritus.* This work, while being conceived as a unity, is in three parts: '*Litanei*,' '*Nachts*', '*Veni creator spiritus;*'

II. *Der gute Mensch,* similarly in three parts: '*Lächeln, Atmen, Schreiten,*' '*Liebeslied,*' '*Der gute Mensch;*'

III. *Fremde sind wir,* in three parts: '*Aufruf,*' '*Fremde sind wir,*' '*Hymnus,*' for mixed choir with violins and basses.

Veni creator spiritus and *Der gute Mensch* were first performed in 1930 under Max Sinzheimer in Mannheim.

The style of the Werfel cantatas summarises all that has gone before and forms a basis for all that is to follow. Example 2 shows the characteristic opening bars of *Litanei.*

The Werfel cantatas were supplemented in *Werkbuch II* with choral settings of words by Bert Brecht:

I. *Von der Freundlichkeit der Welt,* for mixed choir and wind orchestra. (Unpublished);

II. *Vom Frühjahr, Öltank und vom Fliegen,* consisting of *Über das Frühjahr,* (male choir); *Siebenhundert Intellektuelle beten einen Öltank an,* (male choir and large percussion orchestra); *Bericht vom Fliegen,* (mixed choir, three pianos and percussion). This work is published but has never been performed.

In 1930 the publication of the first version of the *Schulwerk* began, and this was completed in 1935. Orff at this time was particularly concerned with the study of folklore. Later, together with his friend Kurt Huber, he became interested in Bavarian folk music. The results are always to be detected in Orff's works. Werner Egk's 'Bavarian style' in his *Zaubergeige* is derived from Orff's and Huber's work in this field.

In July 1930, Orff undertook his first journey to Italy, to Verona and Lake Garda. His humanism, his work on Monteverdi and the

music of the Renaissance, had inspired in him the spirit of the Mediterranean. This journey illuminated those Mediterranean regions of Orff's spirit which, in later decades, were ever more completely and directly to be the focal points of his life. This journey to the South awakened a feeling for the classical experience and for classical form.

On his return in the autumn of 1930, he wrote *Catulli Carmina I*, seven settings of Latin texts for unaccompanied choir:

1. *Odi et amo,*
2. *Vivamus, mea Lesbia,*
3. *Lugete o Veneres,*
4. *Ille mihi paresse deo videtur,*
5. *Ammiana,*
6. *Miser Catulle,*
7. *Nulla potest mulier.*

These were published in 1931.

Apart from No. 3, all these settings were revised and expanded for the *Ludi scaenici* 1943.

Catulli Carmina II followed in 1931:

1. *Jam ver egelidos,*
2. *Multas per gentes,*
3. *Sirmio.*

Under the title *Sirmio, Tria Catulli Carmina,* these works were the first in Orff's new collection of choral music: *Concento di Voci* 1954.

Another milestone in Orff's career was his appointment as conductor of the Bach Society of Munich. As always, Orff stamped this society with his own personality. He had no ambition to conduct conventional performances of old music. His first undertaking was a stage performance of the St. Luke Passion, wrongly attributed to J. S. Bach. Thus the scope of even this enterprise was enlarged at the demands of Orff's preoccupation with the theatre; though it was not in the traditional theatre that his ideas were rooted.

Before Orff, Busoni had had the idea of staging Bach's St. Matthew Passion as a music drama. In his uncollected series of essays, *Von der Einheit der Musik* (1921), Busoni discusses this idea and sketches a stage set. This sketch shows very clearly what ideas Busoni and Orff shared and in what ways they differed. Both were principally concerned with dramatisation. Whereas Busoni approached the problem of adjustment by making detailed cuts and alterations in the text of the St. Matthew Passion, Orff, faced with the relatively insignificant music of the St. Luke Passion, tried to adapt the whole work as a passion play in the South German peasant style. At Munich in 1931, this attempt succeeded beyond all expectation. The performance was given many times during the next two years. In November 1932 Orff conducted the work in the Berlin Volksbühne, and took the production to the Munich Künstlerhaus.

In the darkened hall was a half-lit stage. On the front left of the stage the Evangelist stood behind a lectern; Christ was on a bench in the middle; to the right, opposite the Evangelist, the other characters (Pilate, Peter, the Centurion, Joseph of Arimathea) took their places at the appropriate times. Above this front stage, on a semi-circular balcony, there was a small choir which sang the part of the crowd. On the background above the choir, were projected coloured woodcuts by Tyrolean masters of the 15th century, illustrating the scenes of the Passion—Ecce Homo, the Crucifixion, etc. On both sides of the stage, choirs were grouped close to the audience to sing the opening chorus and the chorales. In front of the stage and outside the stage lighting, was the orchestra.

The staging of *Carmina Burana* was derived from this theatrical arrangement. The narrator in *Der Mond* also came from this source. In his version of the St. Luke Passion, Orff concentrated mainly on the choral settings. The old pietistic arias were expunged, and the text was interpreted to bring out to the full, by pointed recitation, the nature of human egocentricity which shows itself in hypocrisy—an attack on the contemplative man who gives good advice and who fails at the crucial hour. Through this critical treatment of man, the tragic grandeur of Christ is fully realised.

Some examples from the text may illustrate this. The following are the texts of two chorales.

Die Seel' weiss hoch zu schätzen Sie ringt nach eitlen Dingen
Was Hand und Kasten füllt, Und bleibt der ew'gen bar;
Was Augen kann ergötzen Wer reisst sie aus den Schlingen
Und Lust der Sinne stillt. Der tödlichen Gefahr?

The soul will value highly The soul for riches struggles
What does the coffers fill, For Heaven takes no care;
And what the eye finds pleasing Who can the spirit rescue
And can the passions still. From Danger's deadly snare?

————

Von aussen gut sich stellen, Wenn du mit Judasküssen
Im Herzen böse sein, Verräthst des Menschen Sohn
Zu Judas sich gesellen, Du wirst es büssen müssen,
Trägt nur Verdammnis ein. Einst vor des Richters Thron.

An outer show of virtue If you betray Lord Jesus
May hide a wicked heart, With a Judas kiss,
And those who join with Judas Eternal condemnation
To Hell with him soon part. You surely shall not miss.

3

On the imprisonment of Christ, the choir makes no comment
other than:

Ich will daraus studiren	This act may teach the art
Wie ich mein Herz soll zieren	Of gathering in my heart
Mit stillem sanftem Muth,	Courage, strong and calm
Und wie ich die soll lieben,	Of loving all those people
Die mich so sehr betrüben,	Who by their grievous evil,
Mit Werken, so die Bosheit tut.	Seek to do me harm.

After this, the verse sung by Peter on his denial of Christ is
deeply moving.

Aus der Tiefe rufe ich.	From the depth of anguish,
Jesu Gnade tröste mich.	Console me, Lord, I cry.
Ich hab' Unrecht zwar getan,	Though wronged, you'll surely take me
Aber Jesus nimmt mich an!	To live with you on high.

The unsurpassed egocentricity of the final chorus suggests a
kind of religious bargaining.

Orff wanted to project on a screen scriptural texts asserting the
opposite of the words in the chorales—juxtaposing the text of his
verses with pure truth—and thus explicitly criticising their hypo-
critical attitudes. The performance was, however, already
sufficiently controversial, and he allowed himself to be dissuaded.
He did not, in any case, intend a parallel with Brecht's *Spruch-
bändern*. Nevertheless, this performance aroused much hostility;
not because it was not understood, but rather because it was
understood only too well. This hostility did not prevent the work
from making a forcible impression on the young and on ordinary
people. In certain quarters the work was known as 'Orff's
Threepenny Passion'.

Subsequently, Orff gave stage performances of similar works, such as Heinrich Schütz's *Die Historie von der fröhlichen und siegreichen Auferstehung unseres Herrn Jesu Christi*. During this period, he also worked on a Munich Jesuit play, *Philothea*, *Commedia Sacra* (1643).

All the problems tackled here were fundamental to Orff's creation of something new in the theatre. After spending decades analysing, in so many different ways, what the present and the past offered him, he could see a clear path to *Carmina Burana*, both musically and theatrically.

After the first performance of *Carmina Burana* in June 1937, Orff said to his publisher, 'Everything I have written to date, and which you have, unfortunately, printed, can be destroyed. With *Carmina Burana*, my collected works begin.'

PART ONE

THE SPIRITUAL PHENOMENON

I

SPIRIT AND MAGIC

ORFF once said, 'In all my work, my final concern is not with musical but with spiritual exposition.'

There are musicians who consciously seek to express in their music a philosophy of the world and of mankind. Wagner's expression of the philosophy of Schopenhauer is a case in point. On the other hand, there are musicians and artists whose work conveys contemporary spiritual attitudes without the artist's formulating this as a conscious intention. The strength of the 'Weltanschauung' of their time is embodied in their work; it reflects as well as symbolises, poses as well as solves problems. Their work expresses, with all immediacy, the spirit of the time and it reveals, in sharp relief, new spiritual and intellectual experience.

Such is the case with Orff.

Orff's work mirrors the basic attitudes and beliefs of mankind; it gives a spiritual and universal picture of our age, of the modern upheaval. Almost alone among contemporary creative artists, Orff has, in his music, a direct and natural spiritual power, which avoids all rationalisation and forced interpretation; it symbolises the modern conception of the world.

With regard to the spiritual situation of the present, Orff has formulated his attitude clearly. For him, we are at the end of an epoch, and as a man in his old age harks back to the time of his youth, so a culture in its final phase reverts to earlier forms. The simple act of creation, however, is no longer possible when it is opposed by too conscious an awareness of things. One can see, in the works of Stravinsky and many other contemporary creative artists, the superimposition of conscious powers on a primitive force. Orff considers himself a 'sentimental artist' in Schiller's sense.

Certainly, Orff's spiritual form is moulded by the superimposition of a high intellect on a primitive creative instinct. The sharpest consciousness is opposed by a primal creative urge no less keen. They synthesise in Orff to produce truly creative works of the greatest range. And the result of this work is to correct preconceived theories by showing that this superimposition of consciousness on 'naïveté' is still capable of producing works whose immediate, elemental appeal is most compelling.

The crucial problem of creative force and intellectuality is to be placed squarely in the centre of the philosophic battle-field of our time. Orff's work expresses the tension of this polarity but, in the result, its synthesis too. And that, undoubtedly, is its greatness and its significance for the future.

It is the strength of this synthesis of the rational and irrational today that it stimulates a desire for the closest immediacy with the things of both the world and the spirit. Strata of reality deeper than those accessible to sensory perception and intellectual formulation are sought. The intellect is merely a means to this end, as natural science, psychology, existentialism and surrealism, for example, demonstrate. This approach to deeper reality is no longer made through romantic intoxication or the abandonment of consciousness, but through a clear, rational control exercised up to the limits of awareness. The result today is this act of synthesis—a rational placing of signs which point to and symbolise the irrational. With this new form of immediate experience, the creative activity of mind and art becomes again an illustration, a symbol, a sign, of the vital, imaginative world of spiritual power. Man, rescued from the isolation of the individual, can again take his place in the cosmos as a part, and an expression, of the elemental forces.

Nothing is more characteristic of our present situation than that abstract pictorial art, whose search for a symbolism is activated by the same urge to immediacy, should have only one parallel in the history of the world: namely the stylised cave-paintings and idols of the later Stone and Bronze Ages. Paul Klee and the African or Eastern and Southern Spanish cave-paintings show an identical orientation towards magical, i.e. animistic, symbolisation.

And with the idea of magic we touch on a central characteristic of Orff's art.

Orff's whole work is a 'sign-posting' which is certainly not contrived nor abstract, but derived from a creative personality bound up closely with the spiritual ethos of the world. His music has the power of magical conjuration. It brings the elemental and pietist relationships within our immediate range of vision and experience. His theatre places man without reservation into the complete *World Theatre*. More, he makes these relationships part of life and as concrete as life itself. In discovering and bringing to fruition the elemental power of music, Orff leads the listener once more along the path to a familiar relationship with the cosmos. That implies, especially in the sphere of the musical theatre, that the purely aesthetic quality (which is to be identified as the European, impersonal cosmic relationship) gives place to the symbolic quality of the parable, which stresses man's one-ness with the Universe, now as in earlier times. As Klages has said, it is not so much a matter of being as of growth. Modern music, especially Orff's, like modern painting, shows this spiritual development.

The urge to immediacy, which dominates the whole field of rational and irrational activity today, explains Orff's sense of the historical, the primitive and the magical, his humanism, his daemon. But rationalism, which derives from and follows the spiritual trend of our time, shows clearly in his work, which can only be understood and classified from this standpoint.

Orff's historicism is clear proof of that.

The tendency to look to the primitive for inspiration is innate in our time. Today, we are truly historical beings. The periods which provide a spiritual symbolism attract us particularly. Orff is greatly attached to the bizarre figures of Roman and primitive cultures, the world of myth and legends, of fairy tales and old traditions. It is to the simple, the primitive and the archaic, that we look with particular affection and concentration.

All this may be included under the heading of historical sense, which is, today, the preferred distinguishing mark of the intellectual. Wrongly so! If we are vigorously moved by history, then our knowledge of it cannot be a purely intellectual experience. The present becomes bound with the past; the past and present together make up the life of today.

If one knows Orff well, one realises that it is quite beside the point to discuss his historical sense in lifeless intellectual terms.

For Orff, the apprehension of history—the wide field of humanism, the ancient and primitive cultures—is always a source of new, elemental and immediate (ontological) experience. It is his particular achievement to have drawn this experience within the scope of music. Orff is not a historian, in the accepted sense, but a man of the present who is able to submerge himself in the past.

One should not speak of historical sense, but rather of a sphere of being extending through all historical forms and ontological manifestations (see Liess: 'Die Musik im Weltbild der Gegenwart'). The return to the primitive sources is for Orff no more than a return to a deeper self; it is an intuitive grasping of the creative opportunities to expose the spiritual core of our time.

Orff's view that our time marks the end of an epoch makes it necessary to consider his historical sense from a different standpoint. What we term 'new music' today is not original enough to lead away from the thousand year old European cultural tradition to completely new spiritual spheres. It is all part of the ending of the old tradition—as is Orff's work. Only a completely new kind of human being, with a fuller and clearer consciousness, could accomplish a clean break with the past. His music would be something more revolutionary than a twelve-note row—the breaking down of the old tonality—or any other technical phenomenon.

Electronic music, where the human being is less directly involved in the creative process, seems to be a possible threshold to such a new music.

Orff's present position is fundamentally not far from this; his most recent compositions bear a clear relation to the sounds of electronic music. But he remains a great humanist, in both senses of the term. Consequently, the idea of an 'end-time' means to him not decadence, however much the primitive consciousness may be overlaid, but complete awareness and appreciation of our heritage and thus the limitation of all art within the range of human relationships, and within the sphere of the immediately creative.

Characteristically, not all the effects of Orff's work have been consciously contrived; they derive from the immense sources of strength and form in the Western and primitive musical traditions. Orff's art is truly a rediscovery.

Orff's concern is with the immediate—the here and now—the core of being, which, stripped of its historical associations, remains the same at all times.

If this were not so, we would not, today, read Sophocles,

Shakespeare, Goethe, Dante or Plato. Humanism in its true form is the exposure of self, of the eternal human quality, through the classic symbolisations of previous ages. Orff himself said during an interview, 'Sometimes I am asked why in the main I choose old material for my stage works. I do not feel it to be old, but only valid. The dated elements are lost and the spiritual strength remains.'

Orff's historical sense and humanism form a living spiritual attitude to experience, a living attachment to the spirit of all those periods which communicate to him the strongest impulses, immediate as well as indirect. These range from the German Classical period to the Baroque and Renaissance, from the Middle Ages to Classical Antiquity. His attachment is also to the basic human quality of the primitive, the musical discovery of which has given his art its quality of biological and spiritual vitality.

In particular, Orff's humanism is the absorption of the Mediterranean-Classical spirit. The formal clarity of his work in general results from this influence, as does the particular spiritual attitude on which *Catulli Carmina*, *Antigonae*, *Trionfo di Afrodite* and *Oedipus* are based.

It is neither dead historical scholarship nor snobbery if Orff, to a much greater extent than Stravinsky before him, uses Latin and Greek as well as Middle High German, Old French and Bavarian dialect in his work. In the use of old languages, Orff's immediate relationship with all periods finds expression. Humanism here is a reference to permanent values and, through them, an immediate relationship with the present. Wolfgang Schadewaldt has written about *Trionfo di Afrodite*, 'In one great, poetic fugue, Orff's work combines the voices of different times and different peoples. Orff has, somewhat boldly, gathered the statements of the old texts into a freshly organised structure of meaning, while retaining the original languages. Thereby he satisfies the present-day desire to make an immediate contact with the original poem, in comparison to which any translation or paraphrase must be flat.'

Humanism and Classicism are historically analogous. In spite of Orff's humanism, however, it is impossible to classify him as a neo-classicist, if we understand by that term the style in which Stravinsky and Hindemith, among others, have written. To classify Orff as a romanticist is equally impossible, though a romantic tendency is certainly apparent in *Der Mond* and *A Midsummer Night's Dream*. Contrary to the formalism of neo-classicism, his art is marked by its immediacy, its magic. The chthonian strength of Orff's music—a strength similar to Bartok's and Stravinsky's early work—and its power of conjuration distinguish it from historical classicism. Even in his works of Mediterranean inspiration he unites, in the manner of true anti-quity, the Apollonian and Dionysian. The Dionysian quality expresses itself not in a romantic intoxication, but rather in an ecstatic excitement contained within the finest, crystalline struc-tures as in *Catulli Carmina* and *Afrodite*. In *Antigonae* and *Oedipus*, it is the barbaric and oriental quality which gives the work its magical powers.

The sounds of primitive magic ring through the texture of all Orff's music. Orff's classicism and humanism are not so much formal as organic. His romantic, expressionist traits do not express themselves as momentary, foreboding glances into the depths, nor as a nervous sensitivity, but as a lasting contact with deeper spiritual reality. The mystical world, with its great power of symbolisation, resounds in his music.

Orff's work does not belong in any existent musical or artistic category, for it penetrates to the deepest human experience; it expresses the eternal Man.

Orff has been repeatedly spoken of as a magician; it is a title he shares with Debussy. The magical power springs naturally from the primitive, the very root of Orff's art.

Primitivism means today, in general terms, a tendency to simplicity, naturalness and the elemental; a recourse to the appropriate historic and pre-historic spheres. Primarily, it is grounded on the rediscovery of the deep regions of power in man and in history, which were completely overlaid by civilisation. In our time, these regions flourish again, with the reassertion of the basic force of life, the re-awakening of the body. This vitality is not merely an urgent reassertion of life; it is a force which governs our whole attitude to life.

The elemental primitivism which sounds through the rhythmic power of Orff's writing for percussion orchestra is not merely a reference to historic or pre-historic sources, but a spiritual and, above all, a psychic attitude. Primitivism is the primal attitude of the spirit and the soul. It touches, at the same moment, the deepest, most secret centres both of the spirit and the senses. Orff, both as a musical and a dramatic artist, has found this secret point, where the physical and spiritual vibrations interact. He has found there his medium, his signs and symbols, the creative power to appeal directly to the listener's nervous centres. When Orff summons the vital powers by gesture, dance, word, image, and not least, the rhythm of urgently insistent repetition, he advances towards that centre of human experience where vital excitement arouses spiritual emotion. Thus his music appeals to the whole being. Rhythm being Orff's basic strength, Otto Oster was right in speaking of the rhythm in his work as 'Logos'; 'Rhythm is not merely the medium of Carl Orff's art; it is the spiritual foundation of his musical architecture.'

By bringing back to life the basic human power of musical expression, through rhythm, melody, tone-colour and form, Orff has rediscovered an elementary world of a magical nature. He has shown the elemental inter-relation of symbol and experience. This world of magic is really nothing more than the innate, but overlaid, human power, exposed by a spirit whose vision and experience of the world, life and art is free from all schematic conventions. He realises the ultimate spiritual derivation of all appearances.

Thanks to this elemental unity, Orff's work is able to operate a pedal, which couples the secret foundation of the physical with the spiritual life and makes them sound together. Whatever material Orff handles, his music goes beyond the merely aesthetic experience to the summoning of elemental powers. One can see clear parallels between the spiritual attitudes of his music and the music of those archaic times in which it was purely the expression of a cult, times in which the sacred and the vital principle were inseparable and were expressed in the same act.

Orff's theatre is based on this artistic, primitive strength, which the tired, intellectualised art of decadence could hardly summon. It is a spiritual event in the form of a rounded work of art, which unites all the resources of the theatre to make a simple, direct statement. He forces the images and resources of the entire past of both Western and earlier cultures into an incandescent and vital statement, immediately valid for our time and quite free of the antiquarianism which many detect in his return to the past. His return is to the origins, to first causes. He goes, with the instinct of genius, to the most appropriate medium: 'a theatre spiritually activated, and yet technically simplified.' (K. Ruppel)

This simplification, the vital expression of the statement, the working out of the spiritual as well as the technical 'res facta', free from all psychological entanglement, is the work of Orff's life. 'Orff's work is an endless struggle for finality of statement' (Feiler). This finality is the form in which Orff's visionary statement may be expressed with the greatest emphasis and the sharpest outline. 'The nearer one comes to the essence of the statement, the nearer to absolute simplicity, the more immediate and powerful is the effect.' This is Orff's personal credo; and his work vindicates it.

The balance between symbolisation and direct statement is finely controlled by Orff. Naturalism and symbolism are given equal validity. He gives resounding expression to the universal symbols, and occasionally to the specifically popular. The result is a music which, by modern standards, is extraordinarily easily absorbed and wide in its appeal. Within an organic unity, it displays life and indicates symbols. The universality of Orff's art is revealed in the wide variety of imagery within his creative scope. And the combination of sensory reality and inner significance in his theatre shows, with absolute clarity, the truth of Orff's statement that his 'final concern is not with musical, but with spiritual exposition'.

Orff's art, in all its immediacy and simplicity, its ability to reveal the essential while illuminating his world of symbols, penetrates to and exposes the sacred core of humanity. The effect of his art proves, more clearly than any detailed analysis could, the extent to which his creative work is a natural expression of the modern consciousness in its struggle to a unity of the physical and the spiritual; its struggle to achieve a unified view of Man and the world, founded on the progress made in the last decades in natural science, psychology and history. This unity is no longer to be achieved through idealistic propositions and speculations, but through a recognition of reality, of what is in the forefront of life and, particularly, those aspects of life beneath the surface, which even science must acknowledge as mystical.

All modern artists are, by definition, more or less involved in achieving and shaping the powerful spiritual and philosophic revolution of our time. Their works illumine the situation to a

greater or lesser extent. But no-one, within my personal experience, has the power of expressing so immediately and clearly as
Carl Orff the undercurrents of our time. No-one, particularly in
the musical theatre, has so clearly displayed the spiritual basis of
the present, as Carl Orff in his work from *Carmina Burana*
through *Antigonae* and *Trionfo di Afrodite* to *Oedipus*, to the
Osterspiel and the *Weihnachtsspiel*.

II

FUNDAMENTS AND STYLISATION

ORFF's spiritual world has a corresponding musical technique. This technique is highly individual and unusual, even in the light of modern music, both in the attitudes expressed and the form and manner of expression. The fundaments and stylisation of Orff's music determine the spirituality of his music. They blend polar force and apparent reality into a whole. The result is wholly characteristic. The control exercised by the stylisation serves to increase the basic effect of the musical language through a petrified symbolisation in such works as *Antigonae* and, most clearly of all, *Oedipus der Tyrann*, where, for example, a blaring trumpet quintet heralds the appearance of the blinded Oedipus.

Here 'fundaments' refers to the effect of immediacy derived from the recourse to the simplest elements of music-making, the recovery of its magical quality by a return to the simplest forms and techniques of folk- and primitive music. 'Style' in Orff's music, does not mean artistic affectation; it is the essential, organic formula by which his tonal symbols are to be understood. His style, which suggests a comparison with the cubist style of painting, achieves its symbolic significance mainly through rhythm and melody. The tonal effect is built up through formal repetition—in the later works it is as though a carpet of sound unrolls before us reminiscent of the music of the Far East. Further characteristics of the style are the arrangement of a melodic line on a single note and a psalmody which fills intervals such as the fifth, the octave and the second with an elemental power of expression. All these characteristics derive ultimately from the elemental-primitive, which is to say they return to those primary historical and spiritual forms which are such powerful sources of elemental strength.

This new order in music, which differs so fundamentally from earlier musical tradition, marks Orff's spiritual transformation. He functions not merely as a musician but as the creator of a new art form, the world-theatre.

We shall survey briefly the spiritually directed principles on which Orff's musical technique is based. Although his style in no way repudiates the more highly developed artistic forms, it is certainly concerned very closely with the primitive, and the effect of the music is one of amazing simplicity. It is astonishing that such music as *Bernauerin*, for example, can exist as an actuality. The fact that the spiritual attitude is the basis and determining factor of the technical originality is shown particularly clearly here.

The epic-static theatre which Orff constructs calls for a correspondingly static music. It is a logical necessity that all psychologising, such as is called for in Wagnerian music-drama, should be eliminated from the flow of orchestral music. Thus, all symphonic development is dispensed with. Here, one is reminded of the similar principles of Orff's great forerunner, Debussy. What is achieved in the music, which corresponds in immediacy of statement to what is achieved on the stage, is of absolute importance. The musical structure accords with the previously quoted principle, 'To activate the spiritual in the theatre, and simplify the technique'.

In the absence of musical development, as we know it in the sonata form of the classical symphony, there are none of the complications of counterpoint. His music has been described as 'monophonic'; that is to say, essentially for one voice. The whole breadth of sound moves in a single direction, with only bourdons, ostinato figures and organ points providing some sort of counter-voice.

The structure is built, preferably above an ostinato figure, in short units of a single bar, two-bar or four-bar groups which, through repetition and variation, are made to form a complete piece. A terraced structure is developed by successively strengthening the orchestration and figuration. Thus, a piece of music is built up from the minimum of material. The breadth of this readily assimilated melodic-rhythmic structure is supported without any superfluous decoration, and the listener is able to grasp the form in its clearest outline.

The archaic technique of repetition is a basic principle and is applied to both melody and rhythm, which are the main sources of expression. In Orff's music, harmony has no formal function, though it retains its importance as tone-colour.

Orff, here, is in line with the historical process of his time. While in Debussy, rhythm had taken on a tonal function, Stravinsky, on the contrary, had made orchestral colour of rhythmic importance. With Orff the predominantly rhythmic function of orchestral sound is further extended. This is natural, as it is rhythm—and with it repetition—which has the power of affecting the nerve centres in the most direct way; it summons into magical contact, the spiritual and the demoniac, the whole mystical world. Ludwig Klages has explained well the nature of this phenomenon in his suggestion of the closest connection between—or rather the identity of—rhythm and life. How close to the very centre of Orff's musical being goes the comment of a man from China, who, after the first performance of *Antigonae* at Salzburg, wrote in his diary, '*Antigonae*—wonderful—just like Peking five thousand years ago.' The rhythmic force, which is, in Klages' sense, the life force, is the dominating factor in Orff's work. It is expressed through the widest variety of means from the most primitive forms to modern dance, from the simplest folk-song rhythms to 'motor' rhythms. The strongly marked symbolism of the rhythm of Antigonae's walk to the tomb is relevant here. The passage is illustrated on page 48. One could quote a large number of further examples, from the *Fortuna Chorus* from *Carmina Burana*, through the stormy *Eis-aiona Chorus* from *Catulli Carmina*, and the ecstatic *Trionfo di Afrodite* to those vast stretches of sound in the two Greek tragedies, *Antigonae* and *Oedipus der Tyrann*. The power of rhythm to express the widest range of emotion is shown in these examples. As in Stravinsky, the rhythm has an intensity, an impetus, which breaks through the regular beat, often by changing the time signature or by shortening and accelerating the phrases.

Naturally, this power pulses through the melodic forms from melismata, through psalmodic cadences to pure recitation. Even the purely spoken word is bound to this rhythmic power, particularly, when, against the back-ground of the percussion orchestra, it is set to the conjuration of the demoniac world. (*Bernauerin*, *A Midsummer Night's Dream*, *Astutuli* and especially *Oedipus*, the *Oster* and the *Weihnachtsspiel*.) A few bars from the great witches' scene from *Bernauerin* will serve as illustration (Ex. 3).

Orff has created in the percussion orchestra an individual instrument for the expression of rhythm as a symbol of magic. Even in his earliest work, his preference for percussion and for the piano as a percussion instrument was evident. While in *Carmina Burana*, *Der Mond*, *Die Kluge*, and even *Die Bernauerin*, *A Midsummer Night's Dream* and *Afrodite* Orff uses the conventional orchestra, though with a large battery of percussion, *Catulli Carmina*, *Antigonae* and *Astutuli* show an extreme concentration on the percussion section. In *Catulli Carmina* the orchestra consists of 4 pianos, 4 timpani, 2 castanets and additional percussion

Example 3:

for ten to twelve players, (4 xylophones, metallophone, steinspiel, sand-rattle, 2 glockenspiels, 3 tambourines, triangle, bass drum, ancient cymbal, 3 cymbals, bass gong, large tam-tam.) Strings and brass are completely absent. In *Antigonae* there are 6 pianos, percussion for ten to fifteen players, 4 harps, 9 double basses, 6 flutes, 6 oboes, 3 English horns, 6 trumpets and 7 to 8 kettle drums. *Astutuli*, however, is the most extreme example. Here, there is only percussion for eight or nine players (3 kettle drums, xylophone, 1 pair of hand-drums, 2 side drums, 3 tenor drums, 1 bass drum, 1 bass drum with cymbal, 3 pairs of cymbals, ancient cymbal, 1 tambourine, 3 wood-blocks, 1 steinspiel, 4-5 musical glasses, rattle, castanet, ratchet and wind machine). In the first witches' scene in the *Weihnachtsspiel*, in the *Osterspiel* and in *Oedipus*, further new percussion instruments are added to this battery.

A stylistic development naturally runs parallel with this development of instrumentation. The romantic tone-colour of strings against a horn pedal appears less and less. A comparison between the use of strings in *Carmina Burana* and *Afrodite* is instructive. In Orff's latest works the orchestra provides mainly percussion with supporting held notes.

Orff's percussion orchestra varies greatly from work to work; in each it appears in a different combination and with a different function. While in *Antigonae*, the bass drum is the only drum used, in *Astutuli*, drums form the basis of the orchestral sound. *Bernauerin* is different again. A completely new orchestral sound is created by the use of different kinds of xylophones. Orff had tenor and bass xylophones specially built. The xylophone is important also in *Antigonae*, where soft, long-held rolls, played with felt-headed sticks, provide characteristic colour.

It is not only the choice of instruments but also the way in which Orff uses them that is important. In *Antigonae*, for example, the piano strings are played directly with stick and plectrum as well as through the keyboard. In *Oedipus*, rolls on various bass strings of pianos 5 and 6 are played with hard felt-headed sticks, while the other four pianists strike the black and white notes of the deep bass octaves with both hands. This follows the trumpet quintet accompanying the appearance of the blinded Oedipus (Piano score No. 266).

Orff revived the steinspiel, an instrument of extremely ancient

A manuscript page from *Antigonae*

origin. All these instruments introduce a new kind of sound. Indeed, in Orff's music, one may speak of a new world of sound.

Harmony has no longer a functional value, though the bass still indicates a fixed tonality. But this is not essential. Orff's main concern is with the immediate effect of orchestral sound. In declining to construct his music on a basis of tonality, Orff—and

A manuscript page from *Orfeo*

we are again reminded of Debussy—gives his sound pictures a symbolic value. It is the music of freedom. One must go back to the pre-tonal forms of melodic 'models' to find a historical parallel, though we may trace a distant relationship to the present-day music of the Far East in the Gamelan orchestras, in the music of China, Japan and Korea. Orff gives new immediacy to first principles by penetrating through the elementary psychological characteristics and expressions of each musical age to the very world of sound. The value of sound and with it the value of symbol is of the first importance to him. The triad, and the dissonances of ancient music are given thereby a new freshness.

The magic strength of the single note is rediscovered. There are particularly good examples of this in *A Midsummer Night's Dream*. One experiences forcibly the symbolic value of a single note and the intensity of feeling that can be contained in an octave and a fifth. Orff's sound world ranges from a single note, through sequences of complex motifs, to that region where sounds (for example, the frequently used diminished second) develop a rhythmic function or take on the irrationality of pure percussion tone.

Orff employs a thoroughgoing chromaticism only in certain scenes of the classical tragedies; in his other works, the writing is only sporadically chromatic, though, of course, the melismatic melodies constitute a kind of chromaticism. But Orff prefers to restrict himself to the archaic diatonic scale.

Orff's musical statement is primarily vocal. Apart from rhythm, it is melody, unsustained by any suggestion of harmony, which carries the force of his expression. This pure melodic expression must be emphasised as something quite original. The whole statement of the music, including what would normally have been expressed through the orchestra, is concentrated in melody natural to the singing voice. By using to the full all registers of the voice, including falsetto, by using staccato and legato lines, Orff gives vocal melody a new expressiveness and self-sufficiency. A lyrical passage from *Carmina Burana* (*Dies, nox et omnia*) may show his melodic style (Ex. 4).

In this connection, the following quotation from *Afrodite* (Ex. 5), is no less interesting. It shows, in the context of a dramatic aria, the expressiveness of a melodic line leaping across intervals exceeding one and a half octaves. In Orff's music, as in Mozart's, this technique conveys melodically the full tension of the words. Orff

EXAMPLE 4

makes something truly creative of a recitative style. The example
is from the *Canto di novelli sposi dal talamo*.

Example 5:

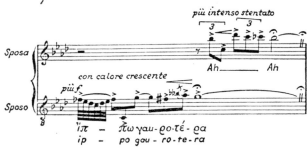

The next example (Ex. 6), which is also from *Afrodite* (*Sposa e
Sposo*), illustrates further the expressiveness of Orff's melodic
writing.

A characteristic of Orff's style which is too important to be
overlooked lies in his consciousness of the instrumental quality
of each language he sets. The influence of the language used on
the melodic form is clear. Latin and Old French texts are set to
melodies which flow elegantly and naturally; German words call
for a spiky, and Greek for a melismatic line. This sensitivity to

Example 6:

the melodic nature of language leads Orff to give the medieval Latin of the *Carmina Burana* poems a completely different melodic treatment from the classical Latin of *Catulli Carmina*. The melody of a Hölderlin setting is quite different from that of a Sapphic ode.

The most significant aspect of Orff's work is his creation of a vocal style. Compared to this, all other significant and original aspects of his music are of secondary importance. It is central to the consideration of the relation between words and music in Orff's work and to his whole conception of music.

Orff's vocal writing goes beyond the modern western conception of music. His conception encompasses the totality of linguistic and musical expression and approaches the old unity of musical techniques of which Plato spoke, and which involved the unity of music and movement, the rhythms of verse, sound and gesture. Orff has brought out in modern terms the 'tonal sub-structure of language' which was noted by Georgiades in reference to Classical Greek. This revival is classical in that deep sense discussed in the previous chapter. Georgiades, whose ideas were almost Hegelian, has said in this connection, 'The classical attitude is marked by the consciousness that God enters into the temple and actually lives among us. Spiritual substance is concentrated in the physical and becomes appreciable by the senses. Correspondingly, the sensory experience is not merely an inadequate appearance of the spiritual substance but a life-form in itself. It is a condition in which the spiritual has an actual physical presence and thus becomes accessible to the senses'. The concept of the 'tonal sub-structure of language' is not merely a matter of the musical nature of words, but shows the immediate spiritual connection between the word and the senses. This illumines the whole nature of Orff's art. Heidegger wrote of *Antigonae* that the work truly comes 'from the source', and that in the *Dionysos* Chorus, for example, 'the Gods are there'. (Quoted by K. L. Meyer.)

As we shall see, Orff's later works, especially *Oedipus*, are the ultimate expression of this concentration on the melody of speech, and they enable us to see his total output in a new light. The basic tendency of Orff's music of language, which becomes clearer with each succeeding year and composition, has been characterised by Heidegger as, 'to give voice to the language of language'. ('Die Sprache der Sprache zur Sprache zu bringen.') Orff does this through the medium of his music, which derives from the basic element of sound in words.

In Orff's developed concept of music, melody extends throughout the whole range of musical expression from pure speech to pure song. Orff himself has pointed out, in a note to the 5th volume of *Musik für Kinder* (*Sprechstücke, Rezitativ*), the great number of forms he employs. To summarise them briefly, they include:

(a) Pure speech in those stage works in which speech is predominant or the music is interwoven with speech (*Bernauerin, A Midsummer Night's Dream, Astutuli, Oedipus, Oster*—and *Weihnachtsspiel*). In the operas *Der Mond* and *Die Kluge* there are also important spoken parts. We have already emphasised that language is always considered as part of the scheme of instrumentation.

(*b*) The first step towards stylisation in the conventional sense is the arrangement of words to a fixed rhythm without established pitch. Such arrangements are to be found in all Orff's major works except *Carmina Burana*, which is written throughout on the normal stave. The example quoted is from *Afrodite (Epitalamo)*.

EXAMPLE 7

(*c*) The next stage is a 'Sprechgesang' with pitch indicated on the stave. Within this category lie both single-note recitatives with corresponding intervals and melismatic forms. This archaic psalmody, which recalls both the 'accentus' and 'concentus' of early Christian music, shows the unity of recitative and arioso in the original sense. Its use of monotone is potent in its magical effects. There is here an important psychological phenomenon. Orff, as in primitive music, lifts the recitative an octave higher as excitement rises. There are many examples of this in *Antigonae*. It is a small detail which shows the way in which Orff's music has its roots in the psyche.

(*d*) This category is that of pure song, the different forms of which we have already discussed. We must, however, say a little more about melisma.

Melisma means the accentuation of a particular word or motif, as on the word 'Zeus' and in the Tiresias, Kreon and Oedipus monologues from *Antigonae*. There are also more extended forms with a pronounced oriental character, such as Antigonae's 'Oh (des Landes Thebes väterliche Stadt)' or, outstandingly, the alternate song of Sposa and Sposo from *Afrodite*. Further examples are to be found in the choruses. All this comes under Orff's principle of melodic expression, which has been discussed earlier in some detail.

Two examples from *Antigonae*, the first of the psalmodic style and the second of the melismatic, will complete the above description.

Example 8 :

Example 9 :

These examples should give some impression of the range of Orff's concept of music. All these forms of melodic, rhythmic, and tonal values which take into account linguistic considerations as well, represent to Orff, in different degrees of intensity, his instrumentation of the spiritual world.

While extending the concept of music, Orff does not go beyond the limits of music, as he is sometimes accused of doing. He has—logically, in view of the intention and compass of his whole work—widened the entire range of music.

This range extends from the irrational noise of percussion, to the clearly fixed tone-symbol, from the sound and rhythm of pure speech to melismatic song. To discover the origins of the fundamental stylisation of Orff's work is a psychological rather than historical problem. Historical comparisons are, therefore, out of place in so short a survey.

Orff's ontological concerns may further be explained in this way:

When a creative artist has penetrated to the centre of primal symbolism and with that, to the centre of immediate experience, his style will naturally show none of the development that the present-day historical approach demands of an artist. Anyone who has penetrated to the core of being will express his vision through a relatively restricted range of forms; his work cannot be infinitely varied.

We should examine music not so much to establish its growth or development but rather to evaluate it according to its deeper spiritual qualities. Orff's work clearly exemplifies the contemporary concentration on ontology rather than history. One must consider his work in terms of his own personality—the self-discovery of his youth, and the need in his maturity to free the self by means of his compositions, i.e. to find the qualities of essential 'being'.

This is further proof of the great importance of spiritual values in his work.

III

THE EDUCATIONAL THEORY
OF IMMEDIACY

I N Orff's output there are two main categories—the stage-work
and the school-work. Both are nourished by the same creative
spirit and both show the same, or similar, technical characteristics.
They are mutually stimulating and, indeed, there is no sharp
dividing line between them. 'In the *Schulwerk* Orff has succeeded
in writing in an elementary, but not primitive, idiom which is
within the range both of the child and the ordinary music lover.
He has been able to carry over his style and "educationally com-
mitted" form of improvisation into his legend and folk-tale
operas, *Die Kluge, Der Mond* and *Bernauerin*, as well as into
Carmina Burana and *Catulli Carmina*. It even reaches into the
great declamatory and recitative scenes of *Antigonae*.' (Reusch)

The revolution in the methods of general as well as musical
education at the turn of the century can be associated with the
physical awareness of the time, as demonstrated by the new
interest in dance, gymnastics and sport. It was realised that the
child's world had its own perfection. The new task was to teach
the child to develop as a personality in its own right, by working
and learning of its own accord.

Orff has posed and solved the spiritual problems of his time
most clearly in his music for the theatre; his *Schulwerk* gives
practical answers to vital questions of musical education. Orff is
not the originator of the basic doctrine on which these answers

are founded, but he was the first to give it practical form and organise it into a systematic teaching method. The results he arrives at are based not on accepted principles and preconceived, traditional forms, but stem from his central attitude, that insight into first-hand experience of life develops, unaided, its own first principles.

The first rule of his method is that all teaching material should be written not merely for the child but from the child's own viewpoint.

In practice, that involved the rediscovery of sources of elemental experience which were foreign to the intellectual habit. Music in its origins was a unity of sound, rhythm, movement and word. Later, these elements became differentiated. An immediate contact with primal experience was conceived as the starting point of the system of musical education which aimed, largely through the medium of improvisation, to stimulate and develop the innate qualities of the child.

Orff's *Schulwerk* may truly be described as a great educational theory of immediacy.

Erich Doflein has written, 'The simple melodies of *Schulwerk* surge with life. Their symbolic intention is most clear and persuasive. Their organisation into an educational course makes of them a compendium of the basic musical emotions. They reveal the roots of the creative faculty.' That is to say that the understanding of these elementary forms leads directly to the development of gifts of improvisation.

A little may be said here of *Schulwerk* in the context of Orff's spiritual attitudes. Wörner has described *Schulwerk* as, 'the educational foundation of the new musical feeling.' Preussner said of it, 'It provides a complete orientation to contemporary music and musical education.' *Schulwerk* is a work of reform by a creative artist, not a theoretician or schoolmaster. 'It makes possible the unbroken transition from the educational to the artistic'.

The method of *Schulwerk* is embodied in the five volumes of *Musik für Kinder*. Its intention is to develop a new approach to music-making, free of the traditional conditioning. In his excellent short essay, *Grundlagen und Ziele des Orff-Schulwerks* (Schott), Fritz Reusch has clarified all the problems involved and has related them to a contemporary spiritual context.

In its origins, music-making is independent of artistic or rational formalisation. At such a primitive stage it has a child-like directness. The unconditioned music-making of child and layman would inevitably adopt these primal elements and forms, which stem from the musical instincts of mankind. With this clearly recognised, the main concern of Orff's system was with the discovery and development of a correspondingly elementary keyboard and its full exploitation. The child's natural inclination to growth and self-expression by means of music-making and improvisation is thereby encouraged and developed.

This is done entirely in terms appropriate to the child. Even the instrumentation centres on the child. The primitive, rhythmic instruments, notably the xylophone, metallophone and glockenspiel built especially for this purpose, are more suited to the child's direct music-making than the piano and violin, with their burdensome traditions and techniques.

'*Schulwerk* is a brilliant scheme for the exercise of the irrational strengths of music. It approaches and makes tangible the vital bases of music in the association of movement and sound, which is the primal unity of body and spirit.' (Doflein)

The system of *Schulwerk* does not itself provide the material for a full course of musical education; it is merely a pointer to the primal origins of music. It offers to the teacher no systematic, that is rational, prescribed scheme or work. Naturally, a general plan is indicated but, as the main emphasis lies on the awakening to music, to improvisation, and the development of creative imagination, the teacher must work out his own means. It is a task which requires complete dedication. The teacher must himself be creative and, like Orff, must recognise the full vitality of music and music-making. In order to develop elemental musical qualities in the child, he must have his own contact with them.

(It is not only the great demands on the teacher which make *Schulwerk* liable to be misapplied. Orff's method has often been falsified by misinterpretation and foolish imitation. It must be admitted that Orff has unwittingly inspired percussion bands to perpetrate some dreadful rubbish at times.)

It is essential that this elemental, unconditioned music-making should be the foundation of an appreciation of the music of all periods.

The value of the return to the primal origins is inestimable. There is no attempt to impress on the child, as the old teaching methods did, the accepted system of the day—in our time, a system of functional harmony. The child thus avoids the preconception that the system he is taught is the only perfect or valid one. Through the re-awakening of the primal centres of musical experience, the child becomes conscious of music as an expression of being, pre-existing all historic, rational formalisations. *Schulwerk* leads the child from the most elementary improvisations on two or three notes to pentatonic scales, modes, octaves, major and minor keys and simple functional harmonies. Having surveyed these basic materials of musical composition, the child is aware of the great variety of possible modes of organisation. He is in a position, therefore, to appreciate the immediacy of all kinds of music, folk and symphonic, primitive, medieval and contemporary. He may even approach the heart of music from which all styles derive.

This education to music, which is primarily concerned with awakening a sense of the elemental unity of music and movement, inevitably extends to general culture, and thus becomes education through music.

Language must be considered as inseparable from music and movement; it is equally an aspect of elemental experience. As rhythm, in accordance with Klages' definition, connects man directly with the essence of life, so the word should be aware of its derivation from the primal logos. Orff attempts to demonstrate this connection by making the music of *Schulwerk* correspond to the textual material of folk-song, fairy story and legend in their appeal to the child's fantasy world. 'Language is less significant as meaning than as logos, that is the approach to the inner language of gesture, absorbed and formulated by the singer.' (Reusch)

This approach is possible only by considering language as something living and quintessential, a unity of sound and spiritual significance. It is to be comprehended not merely through the intellect but rather 'through a sensory apprehension of the word as an audible representation of matter.' (Thomas) Orff is able to communicate his own experience of the total human expressiveness of language.

Schulwerk aims at re-awakening in man, the spiritual artist, the feeling of inwardness and inner fullness. Orff's teaching method makes it quite clear that his return to primal origins is no historical exercise, but an expression of living experience.

This is equally valid for all his work. His urge to immediacy has the sole aim of revitalising mankind in a vital world. As Reusch has said, the spiritual home of the child is not our present technological age, but the world of fantasy, fairy tales and legends, 'those depths and abysses which exist in the life of plants, animals and humans.' It is in this sense that the title *Musik für Kinder* is to be fully understood. In Orff's own words, 'It is the music of childhood, and, therefore, also music for children. Our ancestry need not be sought abroad, but in the child within us.'

Orff once said, 'We cannot contract out of humanity.' If we want to be humanly sound, therefore, we must penetrate deeper into humanity. Orff's doctrine of immediacy thus points one way to a total educational method.

IV

ORFF AND THE THEATRE

THE whole of Orff's work is, in the widest sense of the term, theatrical. It is in the theatre that Orff the musician and Orff the poet are united, as *Die Bernauerin, Astutuli, Comoedia de Christi Resurrectione* and *Ludus de nato Infante mirificus* witness. Only *A Midsummer Night's Dream, Antigonae*, and *Oedipus der Tyrann* use established texts; for all his other works, Orff arranged the text himself. To this double talent is added the vision of a true man of the theatre. The conception and execution of his works spring from his imaginative insight into scene and movement, and an essential realisation of theatrical and musical potentialities. 'His imagination is as much visual as aural, which is rare in creative musicians. He thinks in terms of gesture and scene as much as notes and sounds.' (Ruppel)

The fact that the whole theatrical world is within the scope of Orff's creative gift gives his works their unique quality. The term 'Gesamtkunstwerk' may be relevantly invoked for the first time since Wagner. The individuality and originality of Orff's achievement is the result of an arrangement of the basic elements of the theatre into a new organic relationship. He exploits the full range of theatrical resources, scenic, eurhythmic, decorative and musical. Apart from this, there is a further essential mark of Orff's originality: his conception of a new synthesis of opera and drama. He looks back to the undifferentiated basic theatre of human self-imaging. Orff regards all such theatrical genres as opera and drama as broken and scattered fragments to be collected and reworked into their old organic unity.

It is this rediscovery, resulting from his urge to return to primal origins, that makes Orff's theatrical experiments so controversial. But, it must be stressed, his problems are not those generic to the opera alone.

Orff's theatre has been aptly characterised by Doflein as an organ on which he arranges the varying registrations of sound, words, scene and gesture into a colourful musical and spiritual unity. This metaphor is equally appropriate to Orff's symbolism; all the situations which his world-theatre represent so colourfully on the stage are his 'registration of Life'. (Doflein)

This music springs from the source at which all powers and potentialities of expressing the spiritual as well as the physical are unified. It is 'basic music' ('Urgrund Musik'), as Orff himself expressed it on one occasion.

This concept is to be understood as referring not to Orff's music only, but rather to all the means of expression suggested by the term 'music and movement'. Basic music commands a full range of effect, not only in speech and tone-colour, but also in the reverberating silence of the pauses, and in the play of colours, gesture and scene.

This central principle of basic music shows the clearest differentiation from Wagner's concept of a total art-form. It would be futile to judge Orff's work by criteria appropriate to opera or music-drama. He employed such traditional forms in *Der Mond* and *Die Kluge* merely to express his primal vision of the theatre, and to summon historical witnesses to confirm the elemental nature of this vision.

The subject of Orff's universal theatre is best introduced by glancing at his new ordering of the relation between the theatre of the spoken word and opera. *A Midsummer Night's Dream* and

Bernauerin may offer the clearest demonstration of the ways in which basic music may interweave the spoken drama and the musical theatre.

In *Bernauerin*, extended spoken and musical passages alternate. In Shakespeare's play the text is punctuated by musical fragments. These, on occasion, consist of no more than a single note of percussion, though there are, naturally, more developed musical sections.

Astutuli, in addition to normal dialogue, has words tied rhythmically to a ground-work of percussion. In *Antigonae*, the music intensifies the solemnity of the tragedy. Here is, as Ruppel has pointed out, a new association of the elements of drama and opera. Finally, in *Oedipus* and the *Oster*—and *Weihnachtspiel*, the emphasis is placed squarely on speech. The music is limited to creating the purest and most simple effects where they serve best to bring out the underlying expressiveness of the word. In all the different forms that Orff's association of words and music takes— and the process begins as early as *Der Mond* and *Die Kluge*—one has the impression of an organic unity, not a mechanical, arbitrary coupling. 'Out of this unity comes an entity.' (Doflein)

A further significant characteristic of Orff's theatre is his use of static monologue. These static scenes suggest the qualities both of the epic and the medieval mystery play. They present the climaxes of the drama as a series of illustrations in a picture book. Orff embraces wholeheartedly the cause of the contemporary Epic Theatre, of which Bert Brecht is the greatest exponent. He stamps it with a striking personality all his own. The Epic Theatre is meditative, demonstrational, symbolic and didactive. It forms a contrast to traditional opera, where the music is concerned to reflect the psychological development of character. In Orff's work, musical and theatrical forms coincide perfectly. It is impossible to imagine Orff's drama set to different music, or his music used as a setting for different drama. *Bernauerin* surely is proof of this.

This static form of the musical theatre makes, of course, quite new demands on the interpreter. These cannot be met either by the opera singer or the traditional actor. One needs a new kind of mime, capable of doing justice to both 'typical' and 'static' scenes. The performer must have a peculiar reticence of manner, 'reminiscent of classical statuary' (Oehlmann). Above all, he must respond to Orff's basic music, and appreciate how it is reflected in word and gesture.

Orff's theatre is elemental and symbolic. Like his music and his teaching, it penetrates through all conventions to reveal the timeless bases. It mirrors not society or illusion, as traditional opera does, but the world. The theatre becomes the symbol of Man, of Life and the World—a true 'theatrum mundi'. Orff 'has in all his works, brought the theatre back to its true role of presenting parable and symbol. Its concern is with an interpretation of life, the inevitability of fate, the powers of the psyche and the spirit.' (Ruppel)

The originality of Orff's construction, technique and music is clearly central to the development of this new world-theatre. Orff was led instinctively to this theatrical form; it is not the result of intellectual speculation. 'Orff interprets his experience of life with the clear and certain instinct of genius. On this instinct his world-theatre is founded.' (Oster)

In the world-theatre there is no presentation of the individual for his own sake. The individual case is relevant only in so far as it typifies humanity as a whole. Above all, there is an awareness of the presence of spiritual and demoniac forces in the background of human action. Man is projected against this background—sub specie aeternitatis—as its exponent, its shadow and its sacrifice.

In *Carmina Burana*, Fortuna rules over the dance; Peter, in *Der Mond*, maintains the world order. In *Bernauerin*, the demoniac powers shatter the pure love of two human beings. *A Midsummer Night's Dream* shows the interplay of the demoniac powers and the world of men. *Antigonae* and *Oedipus*, as figures in Greek tragedy, also enter this sphere of the primal world-theatre. In all these works, in fact, the world-theatre is a clear and ubiquitous presence.

The 'static theatre' ensures that the deeper meaning of Orff's dynamic images will not be misunderstood. There is, however, no danger of interpreting *Bernauerin* or *Catulli Carmina* as accounts of individual love affairs.

Again and again, Orff has unerringly picked out from the wealth of material at his disposal details appropriate to the world-theatre's mode of presentation. He is always able to place insignificant narrative details against a mystical backcloth, as *Carmina Burana* and *Catulli Carmina* clearly show. He never lacks for material which embodies the basic themes of mankind, the individual and the universal man, in folk-tale, saga and farce.

Orff's theatre extends to the limits. Behind the sensory appeal of his genuinely baroque settings, we may see the spiritual hinterland of life. Therefore, his theatre is spiritual interpretation and spiritual experience made palpable through theatrical stylisation.

The literary and scenic symbolism of Orff's stage works is, like the musical, close to naturalism and far from abstraction. There is no suggestion of allegory in either the text or the staging. The most routine of daily events, expressed in the most natural language and represented on the stage with simple directness, are infused with a symbolism which places them in a spiritual ethos. This springs from the inseparable unity of all the stage and musical elements, with rhythm in the forefront. As Ruppel once wrote to Orff, 'Your rhythm is so wonderfully plastic because the only metre you know is that of natural mime and gesture.' The simple, readily understood symbolism is part of the colourful scenic element by which the spiritual is brought into view.

Naturalism is, however, strongly qualified by stylisation. Orff excludes the pomp and richness of the theatre of illusion. His work progresses towards ever greater stylisation both in the composition and the production. He concentrates more and more on the simple essentials, achieving thereby a greater spiritual intensity.

Naturally, each work does not offer the same possibilities. *Antigonae* and *A Midsummer Night's Dream* are capable of the greatest degree of stylisation. *Die Kluge, Der Mond* and *Astutuli* may be presented with only a few scenic indications. *Bernauerin* demands a naturalistic stage setting. The spiritual qualities of *Carmina Burana* are unaffected by the setting, however naturalistic or stylised it might be; as a picture of immediate human experience, it has a spiritual validity which is always clear.

Ideally, Orff prefers a stylised theatre. J. Fennecker, Ludwig Sievert, Caspar Neher, Franz Mertz, Helmut Jürgens, G. R. Sellner, Günther Rennert, O. F. Schuh, Heinz Arnold, Hans Schweikart, R. Hartmann, Wieland Wagner, Paul Hager, Walter Felsenstein, Hans Hartleb and others have all contributed to the development of a tradition of stylised presentation. Orff's visionary imagination certainly conjures with increasingly abstract images. His ultimate aim is the articulation of the purely spiritual.

Orff soon stopped giving producer's directions. A comparison of the two versions of *Der Mond* provides an interesting illustration of this process. It was only natural that at the beginning Orff should convey as stage directions all the visual inspiration from which the work sprang.

This point leads naturally to the subject of Orff the interpretative artist.

As a pianist, Orff has an unforgettable gift of making not only the music but the whole work of art ring out. Ruppel has written in this connection, 'When Orff plays the piano, either his own or other music, one is immediately fascinated by a creative imagination endowing the work with shape and colour. He plays not as an actor assuming various roles, nor does he give a merely subjective interpretation of the music. His performance stems from an instinctive grasp of the work's inner structure— the entire significance of its sound. It is as though the score from which he plays contains not merely notes but also indications of accompanying stage action; the notes are symbols not only of sounds but of pictures also. I remember the first time he played to me the great drinking scene from *Burana* ('Bibit hera, bibit herus, bibit miles, bibit clerus'). There was in his performance the whole essence of Bavarian drunkenness, from the feasts of medieval wandering scholars to the October festival of to-day. The remarkable concreteness of his playing was not so much a question of the musician's feeling for style as the theatrical producer's vitality.' Orff's reading of *Bernauerin* and *Astutuli* is similarly moving. He contains the whole theatre within himself. His powers of suggestion are so strong that the scene, the action, the whole visual content of the drama, presents itself. One apprehends the music as the background to this action. It is an equally vital experience to watch Orff conduct at performance or rehearsal, conveying through gesture to the performers how they should interpret the work.

The same truth is evident everywhere in Orff. He works, clarifies, creates always from the inspiration of a scene, a movement, the lively embodiment of his vision.

Orff's world-theatre conveys his experience of the spiritual and demoniac powers in vital sensory forms and images. A true symbolisation of these powers was achieved by conventional settings as well as by the medieval setting for the mystery plays, with its horizontally divided stage. Thus in *Der Mond* there are Heaven, Earth and the World of the Dead. In *Bernauerin*, the underworld of demoniac powers stands beneath the world of earthly happenings and the high world of divine purity. The main and front stages in *Die Kluge* and *Die Bernauerin* are likewise given symbolic importance. In *Catulli Carmina* and *Astutuli* there is a stage within the stage. But even a pure, stylized setting would not obscure these powers. There would always remain a vivid opposition between the powers of light and the powers of dark-ness, and, between them, Man, no more puppet, but a founder, an organizer of his own world. Orff's view of life, its laws and its tragedies, is optimistic. The idea of *Trionfo* runs through all his work, Man triumphant over life and death. His profound insight into the mysteries of life makes each of his works an apotheosis of mankind.

A further characteristic of Orff's dramatic method is his manner of presenting contrasting situations simultaneously, his love of paradox and parodying irony.

The great range of his work in the theatre corresponds to the wealth of human spiritual experience. 'His themes are always quintessential.' (Doflein) Divine, human and diabolic life are forced into a unity in each work. This fullness of life makes his theatre truly a world-theatre. Extremes co-exist, interpenetrate; Heaven and Hell, the most tender and the most chaste, the most coarse and vulgar, the loudest and the quietest, Eros and Sexus, the purest and the amoral. 'Drunkenness is seen existentially, as a near neighbour to lust and death.' (Doflein)

These contrasts are present in the smallest details. Agnes and Albrecht in *Die Bernauerin* are sharply contrasted in the depraved bagnio scene. A more delicate contrast is drawn in the evening scene before Agnes's arrest. Here she sings and speaks, expressing simultaneously two attitudes of mind. The throbbing rhythm of the orchestra recalls the shouts of 'Down with the Bernauerin', in the preceding church scene and so suggests what is to come.

Orff's play of contrasts is a reflection of the ambiguity of language and situation leading to paradox. In this his drama truly mirrors life, which is never simple, but always many-sided. Dignity and ridiculousness live in the same act, sense and nonsense, right and wrong, cleverness and stupidity. Even God and the Devil join hands in the game of life.

To Orff, paradox exposes truth. There are early indications of this in his interest in those parts of *Leonce and Lena* which are concerned with spiritual relationships, and also in the psychological grasp of the *St. Luke's Passion*. Orff is a virtuoso of paradox; he penetrates to that infinity at which parallel lines meet, where the irreconcilable and the contrasting unite and yield their fullest significance. Orff's theatre is rooted in the idea termed by Cusanus, 'coincidentia oppositorum.' Nothing is excluded from the final unity of mankind, nor of the great world-theatre.

This many-faceted, spiritually dynamic world-picture is illuminated by irony. Genuine, serious feeling and true naïveté are so finely balanced by irony and parody that it is often impossible to say where one ends and the other begins. The *Cours d'Amours* in *Carmina Burana*, the trumpet nocturne and the Bottom-Titania scene in *A Midsummer Night's Dream*, the whole play of *Die Kluge*, *Der Mond* and *Astutuli* provide perfect examples.

Orff does not shrink from the crudest realism as a means of developing a contrasting parody, or emphasising an ironic paradox. The vagabonds in *Die Kluge* and, above all, the workmen in *A Midsummer Night's Dream* show this. Here, it must be stressed, is the genesis of the balladesque in Orff's work, and the specific contrasts which he is able to produce. *Der Mond*, with its parody of opera in the death scene, and *Die Kluge* are the relevant texts.

At certain points, the end of *Die Kluge* for example, one is reminded of a 'romantic irony', such as Heine practised so finely.

But Orff's irony is really very different. Heine's negative attitude was so strong as to destroy all his positive beliefs, whereas Orff's irony illuminates the unity of life, with all its multiplicity of contrasts. Orff's own expression, 'ironic naïveté,' most clearly suggests its character. This naïveté can best be recognised in the zither accompaniment in *Der Mond*, which, like the previously mentioned trumpet nocturne, conveys true romantic feeling pervaded by irony.

These characteristic techniques are all ways by which the final truth of the unity of the world may be illuminated. Both the realistic and stylised elements of Orff's world-theatre draw their meaning from his profound belief in a guiding logic behind the apparent irrationality of life. This is again an expression of optimism—the *Trionfo* idea.

Orff's personality, as well as his work, has, in the context of the Western spiritual condition, a quality of universality.

Orff's Bavarian ancestry gives him an innate theatrical sense. A visionary imagination and a baroque love of pageantry are native to the theatrical Southern German. These qualities are rooted in Catholicism; they belong to a land which knows God and the Devil, where the medieval world-picture still has validity, and a deep personal sense of the sacred, a contact with the spiritual powers, has been retained. Orff's personality has, at the same time, wider contacts. He unifies in himself the Latin and the Germanic, the mystic twilight of the Celtic imagination and the clear brilliance of the Southern noon, throwing its sharp light on reality and form. The synthesis of North and South is also, no doubt, part of Orff's Bavarian heritage. In him it is, characteristically, a synthesis of the most widely divergent extremes.

Orff's work is profoundly Western. It unites into a universal whole material from Bavarian history, German folk-tales, world-wide folk material, Greek and Latin poetry, medieval balladry and love-poetry, Spanish motifs, Italian humanism, Shakespeare, and Greek tragedy. Orff's humanism encompasses the entire Western tradition of music and drama. His theatre is based on a historical exploration of this tradition, and a distillation of its very essence. The main sources are the Baroque theatre, Shakespeare, oratorio and opera, the Commedia del'Arte, Terence, and, above all, the medieval mystery play and Greek drama.

Orff's wide-ranging, enlivening spirit derives directly from the fact that he has completely absorbed this great tradition. Thereby, he becomes the Bavarian and Middle-European who, at the same time, is spiritually kin to the Mediterranean, and thus the bearer of the entire Western culture.

Orff's theatre is a world-theatre both geographically and metaphysically. He breaks down the old cultural divisions and gives new life to the whole historical heritage—a heritage which exists in Orff's life as a fixed and permanent value in a shifting world, a force uniting Western man in the present and the future. The elemental is revealed, the whole human experience reflected in a dramatic unity.

The character of Orff's drama is on the one hand Western, on the other, Bavarian. *Astutuli* and *Antigonae* express these two poles of his personality. But, because they come from the same creative source, the same spiritual experience, they stand in the same proper and just relation to each other as the 'Lied vom Bettschatz' to the ecstatic Greek wedding march in *Afrodite*. Orff must be extremely puzzling to anyone without a range of human and spiritual experience wide enough to encompass paradox and contrast. He demands an audience which has experienced life to the full, which can reduce the spectrum of life to the primary elements. However wide a range of contrasts there seems to be in his work, everything, in fact, express various nuances of that basic human experience which comes before all differentiations of time and place. *Carmina Burana, Catulli Carmina* and *Bernauerin, Astutuli, Antigonae* and *Afrodite, Der Mond* and *Die Kluge, A Midsummer Night's Dream, Oedipus* and the sacred plays are not the products of historical learning. Their characteristics are common to men of all times, referring to the very core of being. Orff's world-theatre portrays man here and now, in whatever costume he may happen to appear. Therefore, all his work has relevance and immediacy.

If there is any development in Orff's work, it is in the greater clarification of the essential. This involves making more vivid the spiritual significance of his theatrical symbolism, until the essential experience, focussed in ever sharper outline, can speak for itself. Orff has frequently been misunderstood by those critics who have considered only the musical aspects of his work. Vietta has already made this point. 'That Orff's music is inseparable from the stage is now almost accepted as basic dogma. It is held by doctrinaire musicians of the old school to be also his condemnation. Strange criteria are adduced. Anyone who, like Orff, composes for and with the stage must be less than an absolute musician. One who is concerned with theatrical problems need not have a place in the ranks of the operatic composers.' Orff's inexorable concentration on the essential makes this distinction even sharper. His work, from *Carmina Burana* through *Catulli Carmina* to *Afrodite* and, above all, *Oedipus*, his struggle to realise the spiritual essence of his world-theatre, has been judged on insufficient grounds by these doctrinaire musicians. This in spite of Ruppel's warning: 'One cannot do justice to Orff's creative work by considering only its musical aspects.' As Orff himself has said, 'In all my work, my final concern is not with musical but with spiritual exposition.'

PART TWO

A SURVEY OF ORFF'S WORK

THE STAGE WORKS

Orpheus, L'Orfeo, Favola in musica di Claudio Monteverdi, 1607, freely adapted. Text: Dorothee Günther. First performance: Mannheim Nationaltheater, 25 March 1925. Musical director: von Bülow. Producer: Mayer-Walden. Designer: Heinz Grete. Final version: Dresden, 4 October 1940. Musical director: Karl Böhm. Producer: H. Arnold. Designer: E. Preetorius.

Orchestra: 3 flutes, 3 oboes (1 English horn), 2 basset horns, 1 bass clarinet, 3 bassoons (1 contra-bassoon), 3 trumpets, 4 trombones, timpani, 2 harps, 3 theorbos, strings.

Since Vincent D'Indy's first significant revival in 1905, there have been more than half a dozen realisations of *Orfeo*. Orff's is specifically titled, 'A free adaptation.' Unlike Hindemith, he is not concerned to make a historically accurate revival of the original. His intention is to expose the imperishable dramatic core of the work, with all immediacy and clarity. Curt Sachs has written a justification of Orff's procedure in a foreword to his introduction to *Orfeo*, 1925. 'The values in Monteverdi's score are not exclusively timeless and immortal. *Orfeo* is not a pure work of art, dissociated from a social context. It is, rather, an occasional opera, and the expert may read, between the lines of the music, of the Mantuan Wedding of 1607, with all its pomp and its courtly audience. Monteverdi sets this occasion and this public alongside the myth of Orfeo. To present Monteverdi's work in its original form to a modern audience in the theatre of to-day would be a graver injustice to the spirit of the work and of Monteverdi than a tactful revision with a due sense of artistic and historical responsibility. The recognition of this justifies and indeed enforces the present realisation.'

There is certainly a gulf between capriciousness and purposeful, artistic integrity.

Stravinsky has said about realisations of old works, 'In such undertakings, one must decide whether respect for old music or love of it should be the dominating emotion.' In Orff's case, one must add the desire to bring out the elemental drama.

This emphasis involves considerable alteration. All allegorical figures are excluded. The prologue has, in place of 'Musica', the Old-German Orpheus story of Boethius, which serves to underline the timeless validity of the setting. The characters of Orff's version are: Narrator (new), Orpheus, Euridice, Messenger, Guardian of the Dead (Charon), Shepherds, Nymphs and Shades.

The five acts are condensed into three; the apotheosis of the fifth act and the Pluto—Proserpina scene of the fourth act are cut. Charon alone embodies the whole form and power of the Underworld, and he is given the pronouncement which, in the original, was Pluto's. Because of this, Charon had to be transformed into the timeless 'Guardian of the Dead.'

A few details will show how incidentals have been eliminated. The Shepherds and Nymphs of the first act, as a choral group without solo parts, are presented in contrast to the two soloists, Orpheus and Euridice. The individual introductions of soloists, so characteristic of the period, are welded by Orff into a unified body. The moresca which concluded the work is appended to the end of the first act, so that its jubilation is emphasised in contrast to what follows—a contrast typical of Orff. In the second act, the comments of the Shepherds on the dialogue between Orpheus and the Messenger of Death are left out. By the same means, Orff gives full weight to the tragic lament of Orpheus at the end of the act. The third act rises to the musical climax of the work in Orpheus's big concertante aria in the Underworld. In the third act, by a symbolism typical of Orff, the Guardian is made to represent the whole world of the dead. The use of character in this imposing way invests the Underworld leitmotif of Monteverdi's Sinfonia with organic strength and completeness. The work ends relentlessly with Orpheus's lament for Euridice's final loss. The exposure of the dramatic framework has been accomplished by dispensing with all the elements associated with the wedding feast, which merely hindered the development of the action.

Orff arranged the music as freely as the text. Such treatment is necessary to the ideal realisation and was demanded here by the new dramatic emphasis. From a technical point of view, one may note the modern form of the orchestral accompaniments, and many other details.

The orchestration is designed to produce the sound of an organ. The basset horns and bass clarinet—quasi organi di legno—form a characteristic tone-colour—ordinary clarinets are omitted altogether—as do the harps with the theorbos, which, if necessary, could be replaced by a harpsichord. In the brass, the romantic horn tone is excluded. An instructive example of the orchestration, taken from Orpheus's aria in the Underworld, is given on page 49.

Tanz der Spröden, Ballo delle Ingrate in genere rapresentativo di Claudio Monteverdi, 1608, freely adapted. Text: Dorothee Günther, First performance: Karlsruhe, 28 November 1925. Musical director: Ferdinand Wagner. Producer: Otto Krauss. Designer: Dorothee Günther. Final version: Reuss. Theater,

Gera, 30 November 1940, under Orff's own musical direction.
Producer: R. Scheel. Designer: Alfred Sierke.

Orchestra: 2 flutes, 2 basset horns, 1 bass clarinet, 3 theorbos
(or harps), strings.

Orff's handling of text and music here is even freer than in
Orfeo, so much so, that it might be called a paraphrase of
Monteverdi's music. Orff has a completely new conception of
the text, with quite different emphases. New recitatives have been
added. The work serves as a cheerful postlude to *Orfeo*, and in
order to stress this connection Orff composed an instrumental
prelude based on the quotation, 'Lasciate ogni speranza, voi,
ch'entrate!'

The 'Ingrate' are those who reject love and who now repent.
They are being led from the Underworld, in accordance with the
wishes of Venus, to serve as a warning to the ladies in the audience, and as an unequivocal summons to the bride, in the true
fashion of Renaissance allegory. The work was first performed
in 1608 as part of the wedding festivities for Francesco Gonzaga
and Margaret of Savoy at the court of Mantua.

The orchestration, as in *Orfeo*, produces the effect of an organ,
though here in terms of chamber music.

Klage der Ariadne, Lamento d'Arianna di Claudio Monteverdi,
1608, freely adapted. Text: Carl Orff. First performance: Gera,
30 November 1940. Designer: Alfred Sierke.

Orchestra: 3 flutes, 2 oboes, 1 English horn, 2 basset horns,
1 bass clarinet, 1 bassoon, 1 contra-bassoon, 3 trombones,
timpani, strings. The accompaniment has been arranged for 2
harpsichords.

This famous lament is the only fragment to survive from
Monteverdi's opera, *Arianna*. Orff has arranged it in a completely
modern manner. He has provided a new text for the 'Lasciate mi

Manuscript page from *Oedipus*

A scene from *Carmina Burana*

morire', and revised the musical structure. He has given the work the form of a da capo aria, with the middle section much more freely treated than in the original. The opening ritornello, which represents a genuine intersection of the styles of Monteverdi and Orff, provides a good example of the work's character. Here, as in the *Orfeo* realisation, the accompaniment has been arranged to isolate the powerful emotional content of the great lament in all its dramatic force.

Historical reconstruction or realisation based on modern experience of music are the alternatives which old music offers. The dispute between the advocates of these methods is endless. Orff's Monteverdi adaptations, however, are based on a third point of view: the dissociation from any period of time and recreation in terms of basic dramatic qualities. This important point must not be omitted from any discussion of them.

The Monteverdi realisations were important to Orff's dramatic development as the first full trial of his theatrical skill.

The three works have been collected under the title '*Lamenti*', and in this form were first performed at the Schwetzinger Summer Festival in 1958. Musical Director: Ferdinand Leitner, Producer: Paul Hager. Sets and costumes: Jean-Pierre Ponelle.

CARMINA BURANA
Cantiones profanae cantoribus et choris cantandae comitantibus instrumentis atque imaginibus magicis

Composed 1935/36. First performance: Städtische Bühnen Frankfurt am Main, 8 June 1937. Musical director: B. Wetzelsberger. Producer: O. Wälterlin. Designer: L. Sievert. First performance abroad: Scala Milan, 10 October 1942. Musical director: G. Marinuzzi. Producer: O. F. Schuh. Dance director: E. Hanka. Designer: C. Neher.

Orchestra: 3 flutes (2 piccolos), 3 oboes, (English horn) 3 clarinets (bass clarinet), 2 bassoons, contra-bassoon, 4 horns, 3 trumpets, 3 trombones, tuba (also stier-horn), 5 timpani, percussion (5 players: 2 side drums, 1 bass drum, hand-bell, triangle, antique cymbal, 2 pairs of cymbals, gong, bass gong, 3 sleigh bells, tubular bells, 3 glockenspiels, 1 xylophone, castanets, ratchet.), celesta, 2 pianos, strings.

Carmina Burana means, 'Songs of Benediktbeuern,'—a monastery in the foothills of the Bavarian Alps, where, at the secularisation of the monastery, a Latin codex of 13th Century songs was found. This was entitled *Carmina Burana* by its publisher, J. A. Schmeller, (1847). The songs have clearly been written down by a collector and consist largely of songs and poems of jesters and minstrels. Many poets, from France, Germany, England and Italy are represented. These lively poems, many of which still seem astonishingly fresh and appealing, 'touch every sphere of human activity—church, state, society and the individual.' (Brost) The defects of church, state and manners are satirised, and there are complaints on the omnipotence of money and the decline in moral values. There are also lyrics on spring and love, and dance songs, and the poetry of nomadic peoples, celebrating the sensual joys of food, drink and physical love. Most of the Latin poems are the work of the 13th Century intellectual élite from far and wide, some settled, others nomadic people, who composed and sang such songs.With these Latin poems there are middle-high-German dance and love songs, as well as mixed texts in German and Latin, and French and Latin. The volume, though largely anonymous, contains poems ascribed to the greatest minds of the period, such as Archipoeta (*Estuans interius*). (Only a small proportion of the 'rhythmic poems' are neumed according to Brost.) W. Lipphardt has recently collected a number of the original melodies for the drinking and love songs of Archipoeta in this volume. When Orff wrote *Carmina Burana* he was not aware of the existence of such melodies.

The spiritual unity of Europe, as well as the exuberant life of the time, is embodied in these songs. Above all, they express a timeless humanity in all its moods, bright and dark, coarse and tender; they have 'an indestructible health.' (Schadewaldt)

On the look-out for material, Orff came across Schmeller's edition of *Carmina Burana* in 1935. His theatrical imagination was fired by the very first page—*O fortuna velut luna*, a miniature of theWheel of Fortune. He selected and organised the text with the help of Michel Hofmann, whose verse translations were later replaced by Schadewaldt's free paraphrase.

In accordance with his own poetic idea, Orff arranged the selection into three parts: 1. *Im Frühling* and *Uf dem Anger;* 2. *In taberna;* 3. *Cour d'Amours* with *Blanziflor und Helena*. The whole is enclosed within the powerful *Fortuna* chorus ('Fortuna, imperatrix mundi'). This is the text which the dramatic cantata illustrates spiritually and theatrically.

The work's static form shows its debt to the Passion dramatisations, as well as the realisation of the Jesuit play, with the Trionfo idea expressing man's brave acceptance of every setback, and containing the germ of Orff's general, optimistic theme.

The symbolic significance of these songs, choruses and dances comes into real prominence only when they are staged. 'Orff's first reaction to the collection of *Carmina Burana* was as a man of the theatre, who saw it as a colourful dance and song drama. The function of Orff the musician was to work out a setting for this dramatic inspiration. The mimed events are the primary source of the music, which is, consequently, rhythmic and incredibly concentrated.' (Ruppel)

The early performances of the work took various extreme forms. According to Ruppel, it was performed in Hamburg as a cosmological music-drama, in Vienna as an epic of the world-theatre, in Dresden and Stuttgart as a country manor 'Minne-spiel', in Darmstadt as a Hessian-Bavarian peasant play, and in Berlin as an allegorical medieval mystery play. Now, however, after innumerable performances, a traditional staging of the work has been established.

Orff uses Latin for the first time in *Carmina Burana*. His use of the language is quite different from Stravinsky's. For Stravinsky, Latin is a means to objectivity, but Orff considers it not as a dead language but as the immediate and vital expression of living experience.

The forms used in the work are simple, mainly strophic. While avoiding the petrifaction of absolute objectivity, Orff wished also to abolish in the work of art the distortions of subjective near-sightedness. He was concerned to invest his songs—by present-day standards so simple in form—with a fullness of life.

In *Carmina Burana*, romantic tone-colour is replaced by an orchestration forming blocks of sound. Orff's style had developed from the ripe romanticism of Richard Strauss to a pointilliste style derived from Debussy. The severity and clarity of the Werfel Cantatas (*Des Turmes Auferstehung*) were the result of a reduction in the orchestral sound. Then, under the influence of his friend Werner Egk, his orchestration became richer again. Egk had already, before Orff, evolved an idiosyncratic style employing a rich sense of sound. Particularly at the time of *Carmina Burana*, Orff enjoyed the closest artistic relationship with Egk. Neither of them would complete a score before seeking the advice of the other. Egk's sense of orchestral colour and Orff's sense of form complemented each other.

There is room here to note only a few particular details about

Carmina Burana. The fact that the score is readily available makes
it unnecessary to print quotations. The work has great interest
as a compendium of Orff's orchestral techniques.

The *Fortuna* chorus, with its characteristic colour provided by
piano and timpani is followed by No. 3 (*Veris leta facies*), a
sound-picture of spring. After an introductory bird call, the
rising melody suggests the re-awakening from winter. The opening bars of No. 4 (*Omnia sol temperat*), mark it at once as abstract
and intense. The transparent orchestration, which combines
double basses playing in a high register with flageolet tone, with
high instruments playing in a deep register, makes the symbolic
intention of the movement absolutely clear. No. 5 (*Ecce gratum*)
is a perfect example of the fineness of Orff's sense of form. Here,
the staccato of the first section is set off against the legatissimo of
the 'purpuratum' section, with its gradually mounting undulations.

With No. 6 the dance scenes of *Uf dem Anger* begin. The effect
of the first depends upon the sharp contrast of the genuine
Bavarian dance and a middle section for flute and timpani,
representing the accompanist. The vocal style in these dance
scenes is naturally determined by the gestures. It is characterised
by the breaking down and repetition of words, the breathless
3/4—2/4 time and the galloping movement (hinc, hinc, hinc . . .
equitavit, -tavit, -tavit). This is followed effectively by the note of
the horn, used by Orff as the symbol of distance ('eia, quis me
amabit?'). In *Chraner, gip die varwe mir,* the bells dominate the
tone-colour. In No. 9 (*Reie—Schreittanz*), double bass and tuba
have important parts. The gestures are again cleverly reflected
in the vocal line ('Chume, chum, geselle min'). This is followed by
a turbulent dance.

After the peasant spring feast comes *In Taberna.* This is where
the truly theatrical part of the work begins and Orff's orchestration becomes highly original. No. 11 (*Estuans interius*) has the

pathetic note of Italian opera, derived from Verdi. The rushing rhythm sweeps the singer along with it. The vocal style moves from the free espressivo of opera back to a wild, dynamic flux. No. 12 (*Das Lied des gebratenen Schwans*) is for falsetto tenor supported by bassoons in a high register, piccolo, E flat clarinet, trumpet, and trombone with flutter tonguing. This combination gives the movement a grotesque character. The character of No. 13 (*Ego sum abbas*) is indicated by the direction. 'libero e improvisando, gesticulando e beffardo assai.' In this 'drunken psalmody', the gesture again governs the pictorial presentation, the song, and the meaning. No. 14 (*In Taberna*) is the apotheosis of extravagance. It characterises the rake, the ironist and the parodist. Stravinsky, 'seen through Orff's spectacles,' and a parody of Italian opera combine to form a unity, which is pure Orff. This Italian style is developed later into the parlando ensembles and choruses of *Der Mond* and *Die Kluge*. The impetuous rhythms of *In Taberna* give an unusually vivid impression of orgiastic flurry.

The third part is of quite a different character from the drinking scenes, which are naturally set for men's voices. It introduces a world of refinement and is appropriately given a French title, *Cour d'Amours*.

The first part of No. 15 (*Amor volat undique*) has a freshness and purity which contrast with the sensuality and coquetry of the middle section. Here again the directions—'con estrema civetteria fingendo innocenza', for example—are the key to the psychological interpretation. All the preciosity of the love-game is portrayed through the finest nuances of music and dance. The return of the pure, child-like music of the first part is attractive and intriguing. No. 16 (*Dies, nox et omnia*) is a psychologically penetrating study of persiflage and cunning—but also of truth. Example 4, on page 51, illustrates how all this is expressed in pure melody. The psychology of No. 17 (*Stetit puella*) is equally illuminating.

Tone-colour is formed by high cello and double bass (flageolet tone) with low strings and flute. An impersonal, transparent sound, similar to that of No. 4, is produced. In No. 18 (*Circa mea pectora*) there is a sharp contrast between the 'Chanson' and 'Refrain'. Many of the phrases derive from Stravinsky. No. 20 (*Veni, veni venias*), however, comes closest to the tonal idiom of Stravinsky. The piano, used percussively, is the foundation above which the choir sings 'quasi a cappella'. No. 19 (*Si puer cum puellula*) is an allegro buffo of an erotic character, which Orff used later as a motif for *A Midsummer Night's Dream*.

No. 21 (*In Trutina*) is one of the most refined pieces of the *Cour d'Amours*. It is full of the most subtle contrasts and once again makes its ironical comments through music of an italianate style. A soprano sings in the alto register. This masquerading and disguising of vocal register is a frequent ironical device in Orff. The device is also applied to instruments, as in the use of high-pitched bass instruments in Bottom's scene with Titania.

In the dance-song *Tempus est jucundum* (No. 22), the gesture and the breaking up of the words ('pro-pro- . . . missio') govern supreme. The orchestra is dominated by timpani and piano. The foreshortened echo effect (4/4—3/4) is particularly imaginative. No. 23 (*Dulcissime*), in which the solo soprano tenderly spins out her melismatic threads against an original accompaniment of the low notes of the celesta and glockenspiel with high-pitched violins (flageolet tone), offers the sharpest contrast with the foregoing orgy of dance.

No. 24 (*Blanziflor et Helena*) is a chorus of Dionysiac intensity. The basic bell-tone is conceived as an appeal to Venus. It is a brief but stirring expression of jubilation and most vividly suggests the ecstasy to come in *Trionfo di Afrodite*. The final cadence clearly illustrates the 'cadere', and leads to a repetition of the *Fortuna* chorus.

Carmina Burana enjoyed an unparalleled triumph, and is one of the most frequently performed choral works both in Germany and abroad. Under Fritz Reiner and Stokowski it has been most enthusiastically received in America. Its first performance in 1937 re-awakened the controversy about the new theatre; it offered a clear example of world-theatre, a term applied as a sub-title to Orff's next work, *Der Mond*.

DER MOND
Ein kleines Welttheater

Composed 1937/38. First performance: Munich National-theater, 5 February 1939. Musical director: Clemens Krauss. Producer: R. Hartmann. Designer: Ludwig Sievert. Revised version: (1945) 1947.

Orchestra: 3 flutes (piccolo), 3 oboes (English horn), 3 clarinets (bass clarinet), 2 bassoons (contra-bassoon), 4 horns, 3 trumpets, 3 trombones, tuba, 5 timpani, percussion for 5 players (bass drum, side drum, tenor drum, tambourine, triangle, xylophone, antique cymbal, various cymbals, tam-tam, ratchet, brush, sleigh bells, castanets, chime, tubular bells, musical glasses, glockenspiel, metallophone), harmonium, accordion, celesta, piano, harp, zither, strings. On the stage: bell, 3 tenor drums, bass drum, various cymbals and tam-tams, thunder sheet, wind machine, watchman's horn.

The works *Der Mond* and *Die Kluge* contribute to the general development of the static theatre which *Carmina Burana* inaugu-rated. They also represent a new departure for opera itself. Both are based on folk tales, and the texts are by Orff. The Bavarian quality is clear, as is also the influence of Shakespeare. Orff's original text for *Der Mond* is merely a supplement to the Grimm story, which is narrated in a manner derived from the *St. Luke Passion*. This narration provides the thread on which the static scenes of the work are strung. The text of *Die Kluge* is, however, entirely Orff's work. It is of interest that Orff first conceived *Der Mond* as a puppet-play.

The 'little world-theatre' of *Der Mond* symbolises the spheres of life. Unlike his conception in *Die Kluge* and *Bernauerin*, man is not central. The action of the play moves between Heaven, Earth and the World of the Dead. Peter, Man and the Dead are the actors and the symbols of Life and the World. Orff has used the text of Grimms' story more or less verbatim; only the ending has been altered. Grimms' story is clearly dependent on the Christian traditions of 'heavenly hosts', with the Devil in Hell as the implied opponent. Orff has eliminated this intrusive Christian cosmology. This point is overlooked by many producers, who, by making Peter a specifically Christian figure, falsify the whole work. In Orff's world-theatre, Peter is the magical night-watchman, the *getreue Eckard*, who regards the world as a great box of toys, who holds the law unalterable, and yet views human nature and human affairs with a benign wisdom. Thus he shares in human experience by joining in a drinking bout in the World of the Dead, but in the end he has to apply the immutable rule of life and re-impose the final sleep on the revellers. This symbolises one of Orff's basic ideas. Nothing can escape the world; the world remains the world and man remains man, whatever happens. Here we are beyond the range of good and evil. Peter is a figure of folk mythology in whose hands resides the final judgement on life and on justice itself.

Musically, *Der Mond* may be considered as a humorous aping of operatic elements. The flowing songs, the lively parlando of the old opera buffa, and the great choral scenes are clearly

7

operatic. But all these have ironic overtones, and the satire is explicit in the scene of the Dead, in which direct quotations from Verdi and Puccini, banal popular songs and the songs of tipsy Viennese, complete with piano-accordion, are sung to the accompaniment of a fantastic stage orchestra. In this scene of rowdy drunkenness, the grand-opera style is ironically inflated to the point of bursting. How often this scene—as much as the essential character of Peter—is misunderstood even to-day! Certainly, the use of quotations is one of Orff's favourite devices. He often conceals in his scores references to works of his own and of other composers, which serve, either overtly or purely privately, as connecting links. Thus, in the scene from *Der Mond* discussed above, *Floret silva* appears.

Though *Der Mond* is full of irony and parody, one must recognise also the tone of deep, poetic romanticism. It is certainly counter-balanced by the parody, and it is parody which determines the spiritual attitude of the work. This interaction of opposites has been emphasised as highly characteristic of Orff. The great aria on the World is romantic in the Wagnerian sense. Peter walks as a spirit through the world, while a melody, representing Heaven, is played on the tuba. The melodic line, with its high B flats, is in strong contrast with the scene of the Dead, where a cheeky parlando and an orgiastic chorus convey most realistically a peculiarly Bavarian, brawling, rowdy roguery. Even this scene, where poetry and realism are placed in opposition, is not without ironic nuances. The tuba melody and the lullaby with which Peter sings the Dead to sleep are deeply felt, and strongly suggestive of the influence of the Impressionists.

The world of *Der Mond* is a combination of fantasy and realism, of parody and romanticism. These elements are both sharply contrasted and organised into a brilliant and original unity. The end of the work shows this combination of powers with unique sharpness. Peter has put the Dead to sleep and fixed the moon in the sky. The music has a dreamy softness. A small child comes to the door in his night-gown, and, accompanied by a folk-tune, calls, 'Ach da hängt ja der Mond!' This tender, lyrical scene looks backward to *Der Freischütz*, both in its romantic sentimentality and its simplicity. Yet even here the zither and violin solo has suggestions of conscious parody. This is a marriage of the Romantic and Song-style, of the Arch-Bavarian and Irony. It is the characteristic expression of Orff's 'ironic naïveté.' The finale ends with the child's melody played on musical glasses, as a symbol of the World as a great box of toys.

Throughout the work are interpolated spoken parts, which function as dramatic instrumentation. They occur notably in the peasant-landlord scene, but are most important in the scene of the Dead, starting at 'Was ist das?', through the scenes of card-playing, dicing, skittling and drinking, to the middle section of Peter's monologue. This mixture of speech and music poses the problem of the whole relation between spoken drama and the music theatre, a problem with which Orff was most acutely concerned in *A Midsummer Night's Dream*. It becomes central to his creative work, and even *Die Kluge* shows an approach to most interesting solutions. *Der Mond* is the last work in which Orff uses the romantic orchestra.

A final valid style of performance has not yet been evolved in practice.

DIE KLUGE
Die Geschichte von dem König und der klugen Frau

Composed 1941/42. First performance: Städtische Bühnen Frankfurt am Main, 20 February 1943. Musical director: O. Winkler. Producer: G. Rennert. Designer: H. Jürgens.

Orchestra: 3 flutes (3 piccolos), 3 oboes (English horn), 3 clarinets (bass clarinet), 2 bassoons, contra-bassoon, 4 horns, 3 trumpets, 3 trombones, tuba, timpani, percussion for 4 players (bass drum, 2 side drums, tenor drum, tambourine, triangle, steinspiel, sandrattle, antique cymbal, various cymbals, tam-tam, ratchet, bell, castanets, tubular bells, xylophone, glockenspiel), harp, celesta, piano, strings. On the stage: various drums, small high-pitched drum, small bells, 3 trumpets, organ.

In *Die Kluge*, the pathos and irony of *Der Mond* are transmuted into a subtle play of wit, ambiguity and paradox, controlled with the fineness of virtuosity. The metaphysical world-theatre is concerned only with human psychology. Here, it is an irrational and paradoxical psychology, as the main character is a woman. The text, with its aphorisms, proverbs and puns, stemming from folk-lore tradition, is terse and sharp-edged; it has the literary qualities of Latin. 'Die Kluge' says at the end, 'Klug sein *und* lieben kann kein Mensch auf dieser Welt.' (No one in the world can be clever *and* in love.) This aphorism, though contradicted in practice by 'Die Kluge' herself, sets the spiritual tone of the whole work.

The brilliance of the psychological interplay, with all its illuminating ambiguity, is conveyed with a light touch, detached and unacademic. *Die Kluge* is spiritually related to the Commedia dell' Arte of the Opera buffa. Orff's characteristic stylisation brings out the effect of burlesque to the full. The work's subtitle, simply 'The story of the King and the clever Woman,' dissociates it specifically from the sphere of the comedy of manners. Orff uses subtitles not merely to indicate the general type of work, but to suggest its specific character. Thus, *Carmina Burana* is subtitled, 'Cantiones profanae . . . atque imaginibus magicis.' *Der Mond* has the subtitle, 'A small world-theatre.' Here in *Die Kluge*, 'Story' indicates that this is not a fairy tale. The implied connections are with Eve herself, and all the 'clever women' of the 1001 Nights, and such suggestions are entirely relevant to the whole background of the work. In the works following *Die Kluge*, Orff continues to use subtitles to point precisely to the essential nature of each work. *Die Bernauerin* is 'A Bavarian play.' *Astutuli* is 'A Bavarian Comedy.' *Catulli Carmina*, 'Ludi scaenici', and *Trionfo*, 'Concerto scenico.'

For *Die Kluge*, the stage is divided into two parts. On the main stage the parable of 'Die Kluge' is enacted. On a front stage, this parable is reflected in the play of the vagabonds, which sets the main plot in motion. This organisation is appropriate to the duality of moral truths opposed to one another in the play. The last scene, however, resolves everything to a unity in the mysterious spiritual redemption of womanhood.

The text of *Die Kluge* is not based on Grimm. Folk tales on this theme occur universally. It may possibly be Indian in origin, but it also has clear connections with Icelandic sagas. Orff's text is a synthesis of many different versions. In Grimm, the clever daughter of the peasant is narrowly middle-class. The episodes of the quarrel over the she-ass and the donkey, and the final expulsion of the 'Kluge' by the king are derived from a version of the folk tale from Kabul. Orff added to this material and organised the whole in his own poetic style. The aphorisms and riddles are taken from folk-lore.

The musical structure of *Die Kluge* is extremely simple. Everything is cut down to absolute essentials; everything is most strictly controlled. The style, in which melody on a single note becomes an important element, is clearly approaching *Catulli Carmina*. The repetition of melodic fragments, as well as word repetitions, give added significance to the stage gestures. The peasant's lament from the opening of the work is a characteristic example.

Example 10:

The role of the orchestra is purely that of accompanist, a development already indicated in *Der Mond*. Generally, the music conveys gesture in a most direct way. Orff's well-known technique of repetition here takes the form of interpenetrating rondo-like constructions.

The music's effect is strikingly expressive. 'Orff's symbol is open, direct, almost as demonstrative as a poster, and so simple that it is readily understood by everyone it concerns.' (Trantow) Orff works with the simplest means, investing them with the greatest significance. It is a feat of psychological marksmanship.

The music has, however, a refinement appropriate to the text. Doflein has pointed to the creation of quite new musical categories, originating in *Carmina Burana* and *Der Mond*: irony, self-exposure, self-pity and boisterous drunkenness. The motif for the king's drinking suggests vividly his brutal, sensual and moody nature. The scene of the riddles conveys great artfulness; the symbolism of the lullaby and day-song is equally suggestive and revealing. The self-pitying lament of the peasant is a good example of those characteristic symbols—so different from the Wagnerian leitmotif—which occasionally occur in the score. The back-reference to the riddle scene at the end of the work, where the woman, now representing womanhood, re-enacts the riddles, is a further example. 'Die Kluge' speaks in riddles; she is 'the enigmatic woman.'

The vagabonds are mainly ballad singers and through them Italian opera is again parodied. Their aphorisms, which venture even into Latin, convey the fullness of Orff's irony and persiflage, especially in the way they are introduced. How witty this irony is! Through the mouths of the vagabonds speaks a true humanism, which, in 1943, was very brave.

Fides ist geschlagen tot,	Fides has been beaten dead,
Justitia lebt in grosser Not,	Justitia lives in greatest dread,
Pietas liegt auf dem Stroh,	Pietas on straw lies low,
Humilitas schreit mordio,	Humilitas cries mordio,
Superbia ist auserkorn,	Superbia we choose as right,
Patientia hat den Streit verlorn,	Patientia has lost the fight,
Veritas ist gen Himmel flogn,	Veritas is but a star,
Treu und Ehr' sind uebers Meer	Truth and Honour voyage far,
gezogen,	
Betteln geht die Frömmigkeit,	Piety must beg all day,
Tyrannis führt das Szepter weit,	Tyranny now holds the sway,
Invidia ist worden los,	Invidia is free and bold,
Caritas ist nackt und bloss,	Caritas is bare and cold,
Tugend ist des Lands vertrieben,	Virtue from our land has fled,
Untreu und Bosheit sind	Deceit and Evil stay instead.
verblieben!	

A few details are worth special mention.

The riddle scene particularly shows what depth of psychological insight may be conveyed through music and gesture (the ivory bird, the dice, the king hopefully waiting for a wrong answer, restlessness, hesitancy, certainty of victory). At the beginning of this third scene, the drunken king is characterised by an instrumental ritornello which quotes the reference to Bacchus in Mozart's *Entführung*. Here is a striking example of how action is translated into musical terms in a way which gives significance to both the action and the music. The fifth scene (vagabonds, mule-driver and donkey-driver) with its lively popular-song idiom, folk-song parody and snatches of opera parody, (the donkey-driver's lament), is also dominated by the stage gestures.

The sixth scene impressively catches the mood of evening in the few notes of an ostinato figure. The repetition of words in the lament ('Mit Kümmernis bin ich beladen'), with a melisma on the syllable 'la', has a powerfully grotesque effect. The vagabonds' dialogues are brought to a climax in the seventh scene, studded with catch-phrases such as 'O Fortuna Velut Iuna'. This is a drinking scene, corresponding to the one in *Der Mond*, and the music conveys its character with splendid realism. The scene includes the song 'Als die Treue ward geboren', which was later used in *A Midsummer Night's Dream*. In the middle section of the chorus, which looks back to *Burana*, the text quoted above ('Fides war geschlagen tot') is bawled as a litany. The scene of the dead-drunk vagabonds staggering home, singing snatches of reeling melody and crowing like cocks, is unparalleled.

In the eighth scene, the King meets the donkey-driver fishing in the market place. Here, for the first time in Orff's work, is an extended spoken dialogue against a background of percussion. By this means an intense excitement is generated. Orff uses a similar setting of dialogue against percussion in later works, but

A scene from *Die Kluge*

Photo Madeline Winkler-Betzendahl

A scene from *Antigonae*

with a different psychological content and correspondingly changed technique. The device is used both in Orff's 'theatre of gesture' and his theatrical synthesis of speech and music, towards which *Die Kluge* is moving.

The contrast between the King's rage and the clever woman's composure is the next noteworthy point. Kluge's simple but intense lullaby introduces for the first time a mixed major-minor tonality. In *Antigonae*, this was to become an important emotional device, a force in Orff's magical conjuration. Example 11 shows two bars from Kluge's lullaby.

EXAMPLE 11

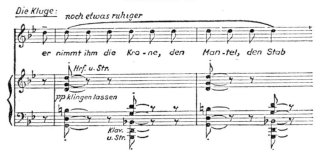

The organ is used here to characterise Sleep and Death, as, for example, in *Der Mond*. This and the final scene (scene 12) venture into the realms of magic. They have been woven from a musical void. The end of the work is dominated by the Taglied, a strange penatonic melody, played as Kluge tends the sleeping King in the slowly brightening light of early morning. This instrumental prelude ingeniously refers back to the scene in which the King first met the peasant's daughter ('Du also Du?'). It quotes again Mozart's *Vivat Bacchus*. The whole scene up to the King's awakening is highly expressive and alive. It is like a vision of the coming love scene from *Bernauerin*.

At the end of *Der Mond*, a child steps onto the stage. This child is mankind, looking out over the whole of Nature, the cosmos. In *Kluge*, the child has grown up and is now the central figure of the work. We are not concerned with an individual, nor with subjective experience, but again with mankind, yesterday, to-day and for all time.

Die Kluge, the first truly theatrical work of Orff the poet, had a great success all over Germany. Abroad, it is the most successful German stage-work since Strauss's *Rosenkavalier*. It has been translated into nine languages including Japanese, and was performed in 1947 by an all-negro cast. Recently, a version specially edited for television by G. R. Sellner was broadcast from Munich. Sellner's remarkable version threw quite a new light on the work by bringing out its intimate, psychological character. His version has pointed the way for a forthcoming film. The work has been adapted for the puppet theatre, where it takes on a quite special charm (Münchener Marionettenbühne 1957).

CATULLI CARMINA
Ludi scaenici

Composed 1943. First performance: Städtische Bühnen Leipzig, 6 November 1943. Musical director: P. Schmitz. Producers: T. Gsovsky and A. Niedecken-Gebhard. Designer: M. Elten.

Orchestra: 4 pianos, 4 timpani, 2 solo castanets, percussion for ten to twelve players (xylophone, tenor xylophone, 2 glockenspiels, metallophone, steinspiel, sandrattle, wood blocks, 3 tambourines, triangle, bass drum, antique cymbal, various cymbals, bass tam-tam).

Catulli Carmina is classical in spirit and form. From this work to *Afrodite*, the classical ideal is the guiding principle in Orff's work. If *Carmina Burana* and, later *Bernauerin* have the northern qualities of the woodcut, then *Catulli Carmina* may be said to be carved in marble, under a strong southern sun, with outlines casting the deepest shadow. *Catulli Carmina*, both spiritually and musically, is concise, resilient and sharp in outline. Stylistically, it is more assured than its predecessor. *Afrodite* is the first work after *Catulli Carmina* to bring these characteristics once more to a breath-taking intensity of dramatic and lyrical expression.

Catulli Carmina is significant among Orff's work as the most radical demonstration in scene and music of the identity of music and gesture. The rhythmic impetus and vigour of the work, which is consciously restricted in its range of melody and sound, is irresistible. The single-note recitatives build up a tension in the listener which the melodic intervals powerfully assuage. The intoxication is induced purely by classical means, embodying the true spirit of antique art. Everything that Nietzsche has said in praise of Mediterranean music is applicable to Orff's work.

It is astonishing that a German artist, in a classical spirit and by means which are correspondingly classical in their avoidance of romantic tone-colour and techniques of symphonic development, has succeeded in stimulating this Dionysian fervour with such verve and lucidity. It is inadequate to cite Orff's humanism as an explanation; it is the product of the entire, distinctive pheno-menon which is Orff himself.

The *Catulli Carmina* were first set in 1930. Orff created the *Ludi scaenici* by adding a framework which gave the work a theme of general human reference. Orff wrote this himself in Latin. His static theatre, with its stage within the stage, is derived from Plautus and Terence, and the Renaissance madrigals and madrigal comedies. Orff was helped in the selection and the translation of the poems by his friend, Dr. E. Stemplinger. The main drama of the unhappy love of Catullus for Lesbia is presented by dancers on the inner stage. The a cappella choir and solo singers, who provide the only accompaniment to this dance, are placed in the orchestra. The old stage directions and the sketch for a set which accompanied the piano score are omitted from the new version as being no longer binding.

The theme of the play is the deep, insoluble problem of the relationship between Eros and Sexus. In Orff's framework, the passionate chorus of Youth, *Eis aiona tui sum*, is contrasted with the mocking of the old men. In order to demonstrate to the young men what the 'eternity of love' really means, they perform the story of Catullus's unhappy experience. But what passion could be bridled by a didactic drama? The undejected, ecstatic call of youth rings out again.

The whole work is 'a double puzzle-game' (Orff). Youth and Age are eternally at cross-purposes, the former meaning by 'love', Eros and the latter, Sexus. Eros triumphs finally as the quotation on the title-page indicates: 'Rumoresque senum severiorum omnes unius aestimemus assis' (We don't give a damn for the gloomy nagging of all the decrepit old men).

Sexus is represented also by Lesbia as the feminine, with Catullus as Eros. It is in this that Orff's puzzle-game is double. The world will never escape from the misunderstandings natural to differences of age and sex. Life—as opposed to knowledge—can resolve the problem. This is central to the spiritual intentions of Orff's theatre.

Orff is interested particularly in the richness of psychological analysis and the elemental heart-beat of Catullus's poems. Catullus is truly the first modern poet. Rudolf Bach, in an epilogue to the text of *Catulli Carmina*, has given an excellent account of this 'lyrical diary'. In this collection of rapid sketches, 'the heights and depths of an unhappy love glow with fire. Requests, desires, complaints, reproaches, joys and praises are conveyed in monologues, epigrams, brief accounts of situations, reports to friends.

Everything comes directly from the living moment, dashed onto paper. It has, however, a positive form, of a grace and accomplishment which can contain even the most daring, frivolous and impudent. It is a fully realised work of art. A note of tender and glowing sensibility—the elemental heart-beat—sounds through all the work. Only a born poet could convey his personality with such immediacy. Catullus, expressing only himself in song, became thereby the first great Latin lyric poet. The wonderful precision of outline, the dry, clear, vigorous diction, the southern logical analysis of experience, the acute articulation of feeling, the terse, manly composure—all the qualities which, in many different individual voices, establish the greatness of Latin poetry, are first apparent in Catullus. No dust lies on his verse; it is as fresh and alive now as it ever was.'

The qualities which Bach enumerates are as appropriate to Orff as to Catullus. The dry clarity, the precision of outline, the vibrancy and firmness, these Orff has as a true antique reflection from Catullus.

Parallels have frequently been drawn between *Catulli Carmina*, with its framework for percussion orchestra, and Stravinsky's *Les Noces*. There is no doubt that Stravinsky is the composer who stands closest to Orff. There is, however, an obvious difference of character between the two artists, a difference reflected in the uses to which they put similar means. Stravinsky displays the exuberant Russian sense of colour, as typified by the Russian Ballet. The orchestra of *Les Noces* and even more *L'Histoire d'un Soldat* is characterised by the adoption of a rich tradition of folk usages. Stravinsky's orchestral style in these works prefigures certainly Orff's use of similar techniques. Spiritually, however, Stravinsky's Russian romanticism is diametrically opposed to Orff's cool Mediterranean classicism, of which *Catulli Carmina* and *Afrodite* stand as examples in theme as well as in style. Orff's simple, incisive, pure Latinate style forms a clear contrast with Stravinsky. Enumeration of Orff's classical qualities, however, must not discount the intensity of his creative fervour. His classic-ism goes deeper than that of the Stravinsky of *Pulcinella* and *Oedipus Rex*. Stravinsky has a conscious aspiration to classical formalism, whereas with Orff, the classical is his natural disposi-tion. This brief formulation is not intended, of course, as a dis-missal of Stravinsky's unique mastery of form.

From the first sharp *acciaccatura* of the *Catulli Carmina*, the urgent power of the *Eis aiona* chorus—condensed to a single note under a *martellato* stamping accompaniment on the pianos—rises like a great arch. The tension eventually subsides into the 'tui sum', which, nevertheless, expands the architectural structure of the framework. The hard, percussive seconds, which fall like whip-lashes on the accents of the rhythm, bring us close to the style of *Antigonae*. The rhythm is given haste and urgency by frequent clipping and overlapping of the structural phrases, which can otherwise be clearly distinguished. The breaking up and repetition of words creates a cumulative power, and the work rises to a climax in the hymn *Tu es Venus*, which is immed-iately parodied mockingly by the old men. The powerful char-acter of the final cadence, *Sublata lucerna*, relates it to the corres-ponding section of *Tanz der Spröden*, 'Denkt an uns, schöne Frau'n'. The introduction ends with Youth's *Audiamus*.

The inner drama of the a cappella settings has been condensed to the briefest form. The settings which were retained for the 'Ludi scaenici' were listed in the Prelude to this book. The separa-tion of the solo soprano and solo tenor from the choir, and the colour contrasts thus achieved, make these settings sharply dram-atic. No. 3 (*Otium Catulle*) shows this most clearly. The inter-weaving of dance rhythms with Catullus's lament in No. 5 (*Lesbias in der Schenke*) is a profound psychological juxtaposition.

Catullus despairs while the old men applaud: placet, placet! In the love scene of the second act, three separate musical threads are most subtly plaited: *Jucundum, Dormi* and *Di magni facite*. In the lullaby, *Dormi*, Lesbia adopts an Italianate speech. Lesbia, in accordance with Orff's world-view, is of to-day, to-morrow and yesterday—the universal and timeless human being. This stylistic point is rarely appreciated. The last episode is one of Orff's magical litanies.

A furious rhythm in clashing seconds characterises Catullus's awakening and despair. The third act begins, as did the first, with the pithy *Odi et amo*. It is followed by the epistle *To Ipsitilla, Ammiana* and the famous *Miser Catulle*. This latter piece has been made more dramatic, particularly tonally, to fit it for the context of a stage work. The dominant ostinato in the basses, with the harmonies a mixture of sevenths and tenths, is reminiscent of Orff's *Cantus-firmus* settings.

Example 12 :

The main drama ends with Catullus's rejection of Lesbia (*Nulla potest mulier*).

Eros, however, is victorious. Youth, unimpressed by the tragedy of Catullus, lets the love-call, *Eis aiona tui sum*, ring out again.

A MIDSUMMER NIGHT'S DREAM

*From the translation of A. W. Schlegel, adapted and with music
by Carl Orff*

Final version 1952. First performance: Landestheater Darmstadt, 30 October 1952. Musical director: K. List. Producer: G. R. Sellner. Designer: F. Mertz.

Withdrawn version 1944 was never performed.

Withdrawn version 1939. First performance: Städtische Bühnen Frankfurt am Main, 16 October 1939. Musical director: H. Laternser. Producer: Robert George. Designer: Helmut Jürgens.

Orchestra: Main orchestra in the orchestral pit (out of sight): 3 flutes (2 piccolos), 2 clarinets (E flat and bass clarinet), 2 bassoons, contra-bassoon, 3 horns, timpani, percussion (small glass or china bell, glockenspiel, tubular bells, tam-tam, 3 triangles, antique cymbal, various cymbals, 2 side drums, tambourine, small bell, xylophone, small wood block, ratchet, sand-rattle, Waldteufel), harp, celesta, 2 mandolins, strings.

On the stage: On the right: 3 trumpets. On the left: 2 clarinets, 2 trumpets, trombone, contra-bassoon, side drum, bass drum, cymbals.

Behind the stage: mixed choir, harmonica, accordion, cimbalom, percussion (xylophone, 3 triangles, various bells, antique cymbal, cymbal, bass drum with cymbal, side drum, large wood block, rattle, brush, whip), thunder-sheet, wind-machine.

With *A Midsummer Night's Dream*, and *Bernauerin* and *Astutuli*
which follow, a new synthesis of spoken and music drama becomes the central interest of Orff's work, interrupting the
development of the dramatic cantata from *Catulli Carmina* to
Trionfo di Afrodite. The different problems produce different solutions, solutions which are organic, not imposed.

In *A Midsummer Night's Dream*, Schlegel's brilliant German
translation has been intimately pervaded with music. The music
is not incidental; it has grown organically from the inherent music
of Shakespeare's work. 'Mendelssohn wrote music to *A Midsummer Night's Dream;* Orff, sensitive to Shakespeare's tonal background, writes music which springs from the text, from the sound
of the language and the magic of the play's magic. The myths of
nature are made audible.' (Doflein) An essential element is the
independence of the percussion, following Milhaud's lead. Percussion provides the magical foundation. The famous witches'
scene in *Bernauerin* is spoken across such a percussion basis, whereas
in *Astutuli*, the vocal part is paramount and the percussion serves
merely to intensify it. The function and significance of the percussion thus differs from one work to another. In *A Midsummer
Night's Dream*, it has a magical function in the symbolisation of
the demoniac world.

With the performance of the final version of Orff's arrangement of the play in 1952, a long struggle with the material was
concluded. Orff first wrote music to *A Midsummer Night's Dream*,
in the style of Richard Strauss, at the time he was working on his
music to *Leonce und Lena*. This version of 1939 took the form of
conventional incidental music. The 1944 version is the first to
show Orff's original conception of the theatre. There are three
printed versions in all: 1939, 1944 and 1952.

Orff's new setting of the play, in contrast to Mendelssohn's,
is generally recognized as a reflection of the authentic spirit of

today. It would be absurd to belittle Mendelssohn's magnificent fairy-music, and Orff would be the last person to deny its beauty. Orff's individual nature and genius have prompted a new approach, have developed new possibilities, which are, at the same time, an expression of the general spiritual and stylistic revolution of to-day. Orff clearly and unambiguously provided here exactly what producers had half-consciously been seeking. Heinrich George commissioned Ernst Krenek to write music for *A Midsummer Night's Dream*, and Max Reinhardt, Falckenberg, Hartung, Mordo and Schenck von Trapp have all made efforts in the same direction. It had first to be recognised that a completely new setting could be achieved only by sacrificing Mendelssohn's music, as it was this music which endowed Shakespeare's play with a romantic, fairy character quite inappropriate to any modern interpretation.

Ruppel has very clearly outlined a modern view of the play. 'Shakespeare's *A Midsummer Night's Dream* is no romantic, playful fairy tale, but a comedy of fearful enchantment. This must be obvious to anyone who has given a single careful reading to the play, even in Schlegel's poetically softened and smoothed out translation. In the play there is little of the grace, frivolity and playfulness of fairy children enjoying, as Puck does, their pranks. Rather are we in the world of the spirits, of elemental nature, a world where intractable, even orgiastic powers are loose, where midnight calls, the owl screeches, the wolf howls and hobgoblins chuckle. The night-companions of Shakespeare's elves are the spirits of the dead, risen from their graves, "In the church-way paths to glide." Puck himself says:

> "And we fairies that do run
> By the triple Hecate's team
> From the presence of the sun
> Following darkness like a dream."

When Mendelssohn's music accompanies Shakespeare's verses, this atmosphere of terror must give way to pastoral idyll. Its tender, tripping sounds irradiate Oberon's wood with light and charm. The abysses close and gentle harmonies are infused where the ghostly horrors of midsummer night are spreading disharmony—quarrelling and jealousy, the tortures of lovers' entanglements, lawlessness and formlessness. In the frightening upheaval of the night, everything is topsy-turvy. Bottom, with his ass's head, becomes the lover of the half-goddess Titania; the most demure maidens stalk their lovers through the dark wood like Bacchantes; the most foolish of workmen feel called upon to perform a lofty, ranting tragedy of love. *A Midsummer Night's Dream* is a superior (or deeper) masquerade, near to enchantment, and not, by any means, merely the comic pranks of amusing gnomes and tripping elves. It is closer to the overwhelming playfulness of the true underworld powers.'

Orff's view of Shakespeare emphasises this weird, sinister magic of enchantment. The world-theatre, which in the previous works was concerned with the spiritual depths in mankind, now deals explicitly with the supernatural powers. The music contributes by transferring its mimetic impulse directly to the actors.

The music consciously responds to the different spheres of the play's events, namely, the courtly world of the lovers and the world of the supernatural beings. The lovers are given musical accompaniment, while the actions of the demoniac world are interwoven with the noise of percussion. The rustics have their own orchestra to delineate their spiritual limitations, as compared to the lovers and the supernaturals.

The style of the production should always follow Sellner's Darmstadt performance of 1952.

We have already pointed out the power of the music to convey symbolic intentions through the smallest phrase or even a single note. This is shown in the first scene (Hermia and Lysander), where the music suggests the character of the good and bad fairies. The wood, which keeps an unimpassioned watch over the whole game, completely uninvolved and yet part of the mystery, is characterised by a fluctuating horn call, which reduces nature to the shortest and simplest formula.

Example 13:

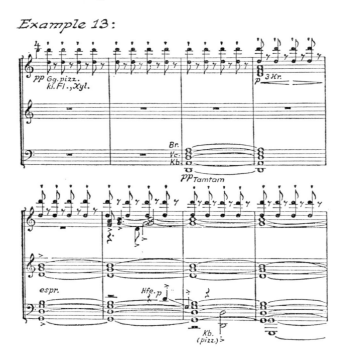

The music begins with a quotation from *Carmina Burana*, 'Si puer cum puellula,' sounded on three trumpets, as a clear indication that *A Midsummer Night's Dream* is wholly concerned with Eros. The tender first scene is followed by the parade of the rustics ('Als die Treue ward geboren'), the realistic banality of which is in the sharpest contrast. This is a self-quotation from

Die Kluge, and is doubly mocking; firstly, the quotation is in itself mocking, and secondly, it is peculiarly inappropriate to speak of fidelity in *A Midsummer Night's Dream*.

With the entry of the supernatural, the percussion dominates. Oberon's scene puts one in mind of the witches' scene from *Bernauerin*. Orff has emphasised the many magical passages that Mendelssohn fails to recognise or omits entirely. A good example is Titania's 'Drum sog der Wind' ('Therefore the winds, piping to us in vain'), which has become a crucial point, where the symbol of the fairies suddenly becomes more sombre. In the next scene, Titania and the fairies, the children's song adds to the general characterisation of the fairies. The inter-mixture of major and minor tonalities during Oberon's bewitching of Titania suggests a mood between dreaming and waking. The same device is used to point the contrast in the scene between Puck and Lysander.

Orff has brought to the Titania–Bottom (Ass) scene a visual concept that is truly Chagallesque, as in 'Ass's Head and Double-Bass'. At a sign from Bottom, the double-bass player in the stage orchestra comes to the front of the stage and accompanies Bottom's song on his clumsy instrument with improvisations in the highest register, using flageolet tone. And the visual concept is in itself significant, being derived from the underlying music of the play. It conveys most vividly how Bottom has been 'translated' and Titania bewitched. Just as they are seen in false dimensions, so the instrument behaves equally out of character.

When, after so much confusion, the couples sleep in the wood, a solo trumpet plays a nocturne to the moon, accompanied by a quotation from *Rosenkavalier*. It is impossible to say here where irony takes over from the genuine expression of feeling. The haunted and unreal quality of a dream is suggested by an echo, and puts the scene in the right relation to the deeper mysteries. The visible reality is thus projected onto an irrational back-cloth.

At the call of the horn at daybreak, the couples stand in the wood, which is still pervaded with an atmosphere of irrational mystery. The horn call, symbolising the wood, is inflexible and unconcerned. The two couples and Bottom must pick their way between two realities. Everything is entangled. And as they waken to the reality of the day, they feel, as in *Rosenkavalier*, 'Ist ein Traum, kann nicht wirklich sein.' Bottom's dream remains a mystery to him, but a quotation from the earlier *Swallow* song elevates it into the realms of the metaphysical. The clarinet runs up a scale of two octaves, there is a single drum beat, and Bottom rushes out as if seized by fear.

The scene in Theseus's palace begins with 'Si puer cum puellula'. Here reality takes over from the dream (the Liebestraum music). Now the play of the rustics is presented with the most banal realism. But even this coarse and banal realism suggests, in its own way, deeper realities. This is the true mark of Orff's achievement. At the stroke of midnight, the magical world is recreated within a few bars. Puck's 'blessing' (not, as before, the elfin ballet) stands at the central point, framed by a chorus in which the elves talk in their own language. The parlando technique of *Der Mond* and *Die Kluge* has been reduced to its simplest terms. The scene, in all its whirring tenderness, is built on a tonal foundation of mandolins, cymbals and harmonica. And the orchestration itself is the final crystallization of the essential meaning of Puck's epilogue.

Orff has recently completed a new edition of the score intended for the Kleines Haus des Württembergischen Staatstheaters in Stuttgart.

DIE BERNAUERIN
Ein bairisches Stück

Composed   1944/45.   First   performance: Württembergisches

Staatstheater Stuttgart, 15 June 1947. Musical director: B.
Wetzelsberger. Producer: R. Lehmann. Designer: W. Reinking.
  The title role was played by Orff's daughter Godela.
  Dedication: 'In memoriam Kurt Huber.'
  Orchestra: (The orchestra must be out of sight in the orchestral
pit.) 3 flutes (1 piccolo), 3 oboes (cor anglais), 3 clarinets (bass
clarinet), 2 bassoons, contra-bassoon, 4 horns, 3 trumpets, 3 trombones, tuba, 7 timpani, percussion (bass drum, 3 side drums,
triangle, ratchet, castanets, antique cymbal, 3 cymbals, tam-tam,
xylophone, 2 glockenspiels. metallophone, tubular bells), celesta,
harp, 2 pianos, strings.
  In *Bernauerin*, Orff's new vision of the theatre is expressed in
the relationship of his own text to the music. Extended episodes
of spoken and music drama alternate, without their commingling
as they did in *A Midsummer Night's Dream*. *Bernauerin* is the purest
crystallisation of Orff's new theatre-form.
  The form of the static monologues in *Bernauerin* emphasises its
similarity to the medieval mystery play. The main points of the
play are illuminated by a succession of tableaux, like the stations
of the Cross on Mount Calvary, in front of which the procession
stops. The whole individuality of Orff's approach may be demonstrated by comparing his work with Hebbel's tragedy of the same
name.
  Orff's pithy, figurative language has the quality of true poetry.
For the first time he uses Bavarian dialect, which alone could
give him the verbal instrumentation he wanted. He does not use
Bavarian to make his work historically convincing, though it
does catch the old Bavarian spirit with remarkable acuteness.
Astutuli and the recent works, *Comoedia de Christi Resurrectione*
and *Ludus de nato Infante mirificus* develop this use of a folkloristic
sound idiom. And the baroque pageantry of *Bernauerin* corresponds to the Bavarian dialect in a very special way.

Orff based his text on well-known historical material. He also had recourse to a 17th Century ballad, 'Von der schönen Bernauerin', and formed out of this material the story of a love which is opposed and finally defeated by demoniac powers. Yet the final elucidation of the mystery asserts the optimistic idea of triumph despite the apparent victory of the powers of darkness.

The subtitle, 'Ein bairisches Stück', implies that the work is in the folk tradition. This is certainly true, however artistically sophisticated it may be. One may say, in outmoded terms, that it is a work for the highest and the lowest classes. It is not folk-opera, which for decades has been thought of as expressing the attitudes of and appealing to a single social class. Orff's work is for everyone. This throws light on the sociological aspect of art in our time, as well as on Orff's work as an expression of contemporary attitudes.

Bernauerin is almost operatic in such scenes as the love scene and the finale. Basically, however, it is a spoken drama for actors. The two main roles demonstrate in the most extreme form the new demands Orff makes on his executants. The leading actress has been entrusted with a single small song. The melismatic song for the solo tenor in the main orchestra gives a symbolic value to the love scene. The solo soprano behind the stage fulfils a similar function in the finale. Apart from these solos and the song of the wandering musician, all the important vocal music is given to the chorus, which is placed on and behind the stage, and is used in spoken as well as sung episodes.

The music of *Bernauerin*, being extremely simple, is most easy to assimilate. The main and front stages are used interchangeably.

At the opening, there is a characteristic static Intrada, and an announcer introduces both parts of the work. There is a typical juxtaposition in the first scene. The depraved background to Agnes's bagnio life, pictured in the sharp-edged French song of the wandering player, to a text by François Villon, is set against the robust German song, *Ein Haupt von Böhmerland*, which, with its bawling, melismatic gestures, determines the character of the con brio chorus, *Wilt du mir ein Ailein geben*. In the second scene on the main stage, a humming chorus, mid-way between music and speech, uses a free version of an old melody to frame the spoken scene of the Munich citizens in the inn. Taciturn and impassive, they sit at the long tables while the music, a Bavarian hymn, also conveys the hunched-up apathy of the scene. The great love scene between Agnes and Albrecht is treated in the style of Italian opera. The repetition of impressionistic symbols provides the musical foundation, and in this picturesque scene the tenor solo in the orchestra picks up, as if telegraphically, the pulse of the few spoken words passing between the lovers and conveys them from the stage above, out into the Infinite. Albrecht's vision is followed by the Bell Chorus, supported martellatissimo on the pianos. This responsorial section has a parallel in *Sirmio*. The ecstatic love-dream music is, at the same time, full of a Southern aesthetic intoxication. Its jubilant sound unites Munich and Verona, placing Munich under a Southern sky.

The bells do not stop ringing. In Orff's music generally, the sound of bells has a close association with ecstatic feelings. Bells introduce the second part, which begins with a spoken scene for the citizens outside the city gates. An orchestral ballad, full of the melancholy enchantment of late autumn sunshine, is played pianissimo. Agnes's Wheel of Fortune monologue in her last scene with Albrecht at Schloss Straubing is followed by a static love-music, with a symbolic organ part. Agnes's touching interpolation, 'Muasst morgn wegreitn! Bleib net z'lang aus!' ('You must ride away to-morrow. Don't stay away too long') is set to the simplest musical phrase. Bernauerin's fate takes its dramatic course when, in the Chancellor's scene, her death warrant, signed by the

Duke Ernst, is issued. The following church-scene rises to a force-
ful climax, with the monks cursing Agnes, the bagnio whore and
witch. It is typical of Orff that, rather than expand the scene into
a full opera monologue, he should set it as purely spoken drama.
This crowded scene is only the beginning of the dramatic
crescendo which rises from here to the finale. The pounding
rhythm of 'Nieder mit der Bernauerin' leads into the orchestral
prelude to the evening scene of Agnes just before her arrest.
Against this rhythmical accompaniment, which is full of menace,
Agnes sings and speaks, expressing two simultaneous attitudes of
mind, the love song:

> 'Hab ich Lieb, so hab ich Not,
> Meid ich Lieb, so bin ich tot,
> Nun eh ich Lieb durch Leid wollt lan,
> E will ich Lieb in Leiden han!'

> I am in love; in pain I lie;
> If I lost my love, then I would die.
> To lose my love and be free from pain
> Is worse than if love and sorrow remain.

She says a troubled prayer: 'Himmelsmuetter mir ist heunt so
schwaar . . . Nimm die gross Herzensnot von mir!' ('Heavenly
Mother, the day weighs upon me. Take the great pain from my
heart.') The arrest of Bernauerin by Duke Ernst's beadles is followed by the great witches' scene. Here the magical world
suddenly bursts into view. The witches, whose lines are spoken
by the male chorus, rise from the floor of the fore-stage.

Orff's witches 'derive partly from Macbeth's weird sisters and
partly from the demons of Schiachen Perchten. Their mutterings
associate them with all the orgies of folk antiquity.' (Moser)
They announce here Agnes's death by drowning. This rhythmical
speech-scene is built on an infernal percussion music, in which, in

addition to powerful tuttis, there are passages where the technique
is, as it were, contrapuntal. The scene is one of Orff's most
original conceptions, visually as well as musically. The orgy of
cursing and scolding derives from the original Litany of the
Ungodly, from old incantations and maledictions. The scene
closes to the hellish laughter of the witches.

The monumental crescendo of the Finale begins with the hollow
sounding of bells. The Finale extends from the scene of the solar
eclipse, through the first climax of the call 'Bernauerin', at the
appearance of Duke Albrecht, to the great choral ballad. The
galloping rhythm reflects the stage action most vividly. The dialogue between Albrecht and the townsfolk becomes increasingly
passionate up to the climax of Albrecht's vow of revenge,
answered, in the most insistent musical contrast, by the people's
surging chorus, 'Herr Gott im Himmel, zernicht' uns nicht all'!
('God in Heaven, do not destroy us all.') The news of Duke Ernst's
death (not a historical fact) is brought by the Chancellor, and
staves off the catastrophe.

The Apotheosis underwent some revision, a vocalise for the
soprano being preferred to a repetition of the love-music. There
is thus a counterpart to the tenor solo at the end of the first part,
except that here the psalmodic recitativo 'Agnes Bernauerin' is
interwoven with the final bars for the orchestra. The old stage
directions for this final scene have been discarded. Albrecht's
vision is now conceived as a purely spiritual event, as is Agnes's
triumph. All the symbols of extraneous metaphysical realities
have been cut out, leaving only the individual spiritual experience.
However operatic the music of the last scene may be, the general
effect is entirely different from the conventional opera finale. In
the end, the work flows into the regions of the mysterious.

A style of performance which comes very close to the
intentions of the work is that of the open-air production at the

Rotes Tor in Augsburg, presented for the first time in the summer of 1960.

ASTUTULI
Eine bairische Komödie

Composed: 1945/1946. First performance: Münchner Kammerspiele, 20 October 1953. Musical director: K. List. Producer: Hans Schweikart. Designer: H. Jürgens.

Orchestra: percussion for 8 to 9 players (3 kettle drums, xylophone, 1 pair of hand-drums (bongo), 2 side drums, 3 tenor drums, tambourine, bass drum, bass drum with cymbal, cymbal, 1 pair of cymbals, 3 wood blocks, steinspiel, 4 to 5 musical glasses (these are played with the tips of the fingers on the rim. They are tuned to adjacent diminished seconds at a very high pitch), rattle, castanets, ratchet, wind-machine.

On the stage: a suspended cymbal.

Astutuli is the Satyr-play to *Bernauerin*, and, in the same spirit of 'world-theatre', its final significance is metaphysical. The magical demoniac dance which ends, but does not resolve the work, makes that clear. The text of *Astutuli* is Orff's own, and is again in a vigorous and robust Bavarian dialect. Like *Bernauerin*, it is a work for actors. Orff placed no value on the actuality of the work as a satire on mass suggestion and illusionism. Consequently, there were eight years between composition and first performance.

'O vos, Astutuli', calls the trickster as he makes off after fleecing the local farmers. 'Astutuli'—Orff the humanist has revived the term—is derived from the Latin 'astutus' (astute, crafty) and here refers to the too clever who, being basically stupid, are easy prey to every humbug who can play on their vanity. Following the example of Cervantes, Orff has in *Astutuli*, given literary elevation to what is, in effect, an improvised farce.

A scene in one of Cervantes' theatrical Interludes is the ultimate source of *Astutuli*. Orff's tricksters are true descendants of the vagabonds of *Die Kluge;* they chatter away right up to the scene of their departure, 'Applaudite.'

The text is coarse and vulgar and so too is the meaning. 'Wenn i di heunt noch hab, frag i nach morgen nix, brauch kan kokanisch Gwand und a kein andres net, lieg i ganz ohne Gwand bei dir im Bett!' (If I still have you to-day, I do not bother about to-morrow. I don't need flashy clothes, or any other kind either. I can lie without clothes with you in bed.) But the magical, spiritual background—the perspective of the world-theatre—commands absolute attention: the world is under the influence of the demoniac powers, powers which break out, now as in the past, in mass suggestion and illusionism, which are eternally kindled by trickery, which steal men's goods as well as their souls, and then, turning trickster themselves, bring men to the debasement of surpassing greed, and finally leave them swaying in the vacuity of illusion.

The music is stylistically extreme. In this 'Sprechstück', the 'music of language' develops its own free, rhythmic forms in solos and choral counterpoint. The conventional stave is used only in the hummed chorus of the finale and in the chorus, sung in expectation of a vision of the future, 'D'Zeit lasst si Zeit' (Time takes its time). This is a simple tonic-dominant alternation in Bavarian dance rhythm.

The melody of speech governs the score. It follows, therefore, that rhythm is the dominating element. Gesture is the crucial factor in determining language, sound and movement. There is a clear derivation from the witches' scene of *Bernauerin*. The different role of the percussion in the two scenes has already been suggested in connection with the general problem of *A Midsummer Night's Dream*. *Astutuli* proceeds from the speaking voice, and the quasi-vocal parts are intensified by a percussion base. The scenes have a rondo-like construction, building up to a powerful crescendo.

It is, of course, neither snobbery nor creative poverty which led Orff to this style of composition. The work realises in a quite individual way, the synthesis of spoken drama and music-theatre, with a characteristic concentration on the essential. It represents also an experiment with a new range of sound together with the music of language.

ANTIGONAE
Ein Trauerspiel des Sophokles von Friedrich Hölderlin

Composed 1947/48. First performance: Felsenreitschule, 9 August 1949, as part of the Salzburg Festival. Musical director: Ferenc Fricsay. Producer: O. F. Schuh. Designer: C. Neher.
  Antigonae: R. Fischer. Kreon: H. Uhde.
  Orchestra: 6 Grand pianos, also played with drum-sticks and plectrum, 4 harps, 9 double basses, 6 flutes (piccolos), 6 oboes (3 English horns), 6 trumpets with mutes, 7-8 timpani (one tuned to high A), percussion for ten to fifteen players (steinspiel (soprano), 2-3 xylophones 2 (1) trough-xylophones (soprano), 6 (4) trough-xylphones (tenor), 2 (1) trough-xylophones (bass), 1 small wood-block, 1 large African wood-block, 2 bells, 3 glockenspiels, 4 pairs of cymbals, 3 Turkish cymbals, 3 pairs of Turkish cymbals, 1 small anvil, 3 triangles, 2 bass drums, 6 tambourines, 6 pairs of castanets, 10 large Javanese gongs.) The orchestra should, if possible, not be visible to the audience.

In spirit, all Orff's work is ultimately derived from Greek tragedy. His world-theatre, in some works truly Antique, in others closer to the medieval mystery play, clearly indicates this.

Antigonae was planned as early as 1940, and a first draft was written in 1943. It is a setting of Hölderlin's version of the Sophocles tragedy, and Orff's intention was to elevate its hieratic structure to the full solemnity of the cult theatre. This approach is quite different from that which led Strauss to Wilde's *Salome* or to Hofmannsthal's *Elektra*. Orff was concerned solely with the presentation and spiritual vitalisation of Sophocles' tragedy, which he set to music word for word. Orff himself said: 'From the very beginning, I saw that there was nothing to add to Sophocles' text. My task was to interpret it in a contemporary medium. *Antigonae* is not a work for the opera repertory; it is a ceremonial, a cult work. I consider my work merely as an interpretation of Sophocles' play for our time; his is the significant contribution, not mine. Behind him lies a whole world.' (quoted by Vietta.) The work gives one a full sense of the scope of Orff's 'spiritual exposition'.

Hölderlin's translation is a creative achievement in its own right. It re-created Sophocles' work from the deepest lived experience, placing it in a Western spiritual context. 'The sphinx-like solidity, the static self-containment of the Greek tragedy has been touched with a burning finger, so that it erupts and flows volcanically in the language of the West.' (Georgiades) For him, Sophocles' tragedy was 'a remnant of divinity' saved, and newly awakened for us. It was, to Hölderlin, freshly discovered Divine writ. To communicate the religious message that the tragedies contain, it is necessary not so much to translate *Antigonae* as to transpose it into the religious key of the 'Hesperides' (Reinhardt). This involves expressing a sense of the spiritual enormities of the cthonic, the 'barbaric' and 'oriental' vision, in uncertain, stammering hymns. But there is also the ecstatic experience of immediacy which has a Prophet-like closeness to God. Spirit and magic bind Hölderlin's dark language.

One can understand how clearly Orff would recognise his

affinity with the Hölderlin of the Sophocles translations. 'Where language works on such a deep level, its roots must be fed from a correspondingly deep musical spring.' (Keller)

From Orff's point of view, the essential quality of Hölderlin's re-creation was that it remained an inspired first idea—a scheme for adapting the tragedy to a Western spiritual context, which, in order to be an effective and valid realisation for our time, needed ceremonial music such as Orff provided. 'The creative stimulus of Hölderlin's work lies in its apparent limitation. Orff's infallible instinct took him to a translation which conveys the significance of Sophocles to the Western spirit with a power which derives from its very fragmentory quality.' (Georgiades). Orff adapted the work for the present-day theatre, emphasising that mysterious, magical background which Hölderlin had revealed in Sophocles' *Antigonae*.

The spiritual and technical qualities of *Antigonae* are entirely characteristic of Orff's style, the essential elements of which are seen at their most pure in this monumental work. It is in *Oedipus* that they are developed to their logical conclusion. The synthesis of spoken drama and the music-theatre is here achieved through a psalmodic form of expression, which demands Orff's new kind of actor-singer for its interpretation. Rhythm here has a constructional rather than a motive power. The melodic symbols, frequently melismatic, the complete and clear significance of what is expressed—Orff's characteristic sign-posting—all those phenomena of Orff's musical and theatrical language which were discussed in general terms in the first part of the book, are present in this work in the purest form. There is no inessential sensory appeal; everything is directly spiritual. The powerful tensions of the drama, which are affirmed rather than pessimistically evaded, are contained within the stony, petrified forms of the spiritual stylisation, without losing any of their fire and intensity. The special and unique instrumentation follows from this spiritualised intensity. The magical basis of the theatre is most clearly exposed, and yet it is, at the same time, living theatre, in which foreground and background come into mutually illuminating contact.

W. Keller has written an excellent introduction to *Antigonae*, published by Schott. Only a few outstanding points need, therefore, be mentioned here. The most important of these are the great Kreon scenes, the soliloquies and the dialogues with Antigonae, Haemon and Tiresias, Antigonae's main scenes, and the choral scenes. In the scene between Ismene and Antigonae, the steinspiel, playing in seconds and double-seconds, is introduced with dazzling effect. The sisters' dialogue builds up to the pounding instrumental introduction of the monumental chorus, 'O Blik der Sonne'. This is a terraced structure, the orchestration becoming correspondingly more intense at each stage. Here we have another example of the architectural value of Orff's massive, monumental constructions. Kreon is introduced by a glissando, an effect particularly associated with *Afrodite*. At the same time, the Watchman is characterised by a piercing sound with a xylophone after-note. The repetition of these symbols gives strength to the stylisation. The single-note recitative, which is in itself colourless, widens out into arioso or to speech rhythms set in widely leaping intervals, to melismatic and chromatic melody, according to the emotional or symbolic demands of the moment.

The chorus 'Ungeheuer ist viel' begins the second part. It develops powerfully from the frequently used device of major-minor fluctuations. Here they symbolise vividly 'the tragic dual role which Man is condemned to play.' (Keller) The following scene, between Kreon and the Watchman who betrayed Antigonae, has a Bach-like use of symbolic tone-colouring at such points as 'und weinet auf'. In the scene between Kreon and Antigonae which follows, Antigonae's profession of faith in the

eternal laws is accompanied by the powerful rhythmic figure
which represents her walk to the grave. Her speech climbs,
'fanatico', two octaves at the words, 'Zum Hasse nicht, zur
Liebe bin ich.' ('I live not for hatred but for love.') 'O, liebster,
Haemon, wie entehrt er dich!' ('Oh dearest Haemon, how he
dishonours you.') marks another climax. The recitative starts with
a leap of a twelfth and then falls from the high A to a low C.
The final ritornello combines all the tonal symbols of the scene,
unified in a way similar to that of 'Invocazione dell' Imeneo' from
Afrodite. The chorus, 'Glückselige solcher Zeiten' is a tone poem
symbolising wind and water. A vigorous instrumental interlude
leads to the Kreon–Haemon scene. Haemon, the weakest and
simplest character in the tragedy, is shown in stiffening opposition
to his father in the wide-ranging intervals of his gradually intensifying melodic line. He leaves to the accompaniment of the
hammered top notes of the pianos. After Kreon has passed sen-
tence on Antigonae, against a pounding bass figure which is

EXAMPLE 14

heard again at the end of the tragedy, the chorus, 'Geist der Liebe'
rises to the lyrical climax of the whole work. It has a loose strophic
form; the chorus sings a cappella and in thirds, with a certain
interweaving of voices (Ex. 14). Its calm detachment distinguishes
it from all the other choral parts of the work.

The instruments are introduced successively and each has its
symbolic significance. The flutes, which appear for the first time
at the words 'die göttliche Schönheit', represent bird-song.
Antigonae appears to pounding rhythms which point to a tragic
ending. In her dialogue with the chorus, a recitative on the note
D has, though a monotone, the expressive power of ritual. It
begins with the fearful cry, 'Weh, närrisch machen sie mich!'
(Oh, what a fool they make of me.) From this, the recitative rises
chromatically to its greatest pitch of intensity at 'Jo! Jo! mein
Bruder!' Her cry, 'O Grab, o Brautbett!' plunges down over two
octaves. Against the powerful rhythm of the sacred dance, full
of emanations of the cthonic, Antigonae paces towards the tomb,
while Keron's death-scream rings out.

The fourth part begins with Antigonae's farewell lament, one
of the most impressive of the great melismatic settings in the
score. It is followed by a petrified, monumental choral dance in
which the chorus sings to Antigonae of the divine law. The metric
rigidity of this chorus is in the sharpest contrast to the free,
swinging relaxedness of 'Geist der Liebe'. Each strophe develops
an overwhelming intensity, and ends in an orgiastic undulating
figure. The Tiresias scene has been made immensely expressive.
Its use of melisma gives us one of the best examples of the expressive power of pure melody in the whole of Orff's work. It
begins with the sound of muted trumpets playing in diminished
seconds. As the excitement grows, the orchestral colour becomes
increasingly tense and harsh, and the vocal line more melismatic.
The use of melisma in *Afrodite*, especially in the scene of the

bridal chamber, derives from here, even though the emotions it expresses are so different. Characteristically, the Tiresias melisma is re-introduced at each of his entries, and thus constitutes an element of the strophic, rondo-like structure of the scene. The more Kreon contradicts and challenges Tiresias, the shriller the sound of the diminished seconds becomes. Thus, the total structure of the scene is most impressively developed up to the point at which Kreon is left alone, shattered by the prophecies. After a short spoken scene with the chorus, Kreon, helpless and perplexed, breaks out into the sudden climax of the melisma 'O mir!' This is a good example of the certainty with which Orff can mobilise the basic sound patterns of language.

The following chorus, 'Nahmenschöpfer-Chor', develops from a single-note recitative to an ecstatic hymn ('Jo! Du! in Feuer wandelnd!'). It leads to the scene between Euridice and the Messenger, with its finely woven symbolism, and to the first part of Kreon's great monologue. This begins with a glissando, and ranges, 'intenso appassionato lamento', through the heights and depths of desperation and contrition. The music is built on oscillating, chromatic figures in the highest ranges of the voice (Ex. 15).

EXAMPLE 15

The news of Euridice's death leads to the second part of the monologue, an outbreak of desperation. Realistically, the lament subsides finally into whimpering and then into speech. Just before Kreon's exit, the emotional tension suddenly rises again: 'O komm!—Erscheine meiner Verhängnisse schönstes, den endlichen Tag mir bringend, den letzten . . .' (Come, the best part of my destiny, bringing my last day.')

The basic idea of the drama is pronounced by the Messenger: 'Von vorgesetztem Verhängnis hat kein Sterblicher Befreiung!' ('No mortal can escape his pre-ordained fate.') The Chorus, after a final comment, turns to go. The last sound is a bottom C played pianissimo on the pianos.

TRIONFO DI AFRODITE
Concerto scenico

Composed 1950/51. First performance: Scala, Milan, 13 February 1953. Musical director: Herbert von Karajan. Producer: Herbert von Karajan. Designer: J. Fennecker. This Milan production was the first performance of *Trionfi*, which consists of *Carmina Burana*, *Catulli Carmina* and *Trionfo di Afrodite*. First Concert performance of *Trionfo di Afrodite*: Munich, 5 March 1953. Conductor: Eugen Jochum. First German production of *Trionfi*: Staatstheater Stuttgart, 10 March 1953. Musical director: Ferdinand Leitner. Producer: Heinz Arnold. Designer: Gerd Richter.

Orchestra: 3 flutes (piccolos), 3 oboes (2 English horns), 3 clarinets, 3 bassoons, 1 contra-bassoon, 6 horns, 3 trumpets, 3 trombones, 2 tubas, 2 harps, 3 guitars, 3 pianos, strings, percussion (6 kettle drums, 3 glockenspiels, 1 xylophone, 1 marimbaphone, 1 tenor xylophone, 4 wood blocks, castanets, triangle, 4 various cymbals, tam-tam, tubular bells, tambourine, 2 side drums (with and without snares), 2 bass drums, rattle). Behind the stage: harp,

2 pianos, violins, 2 violas, 1 double bass, glockenspiel, xylophone, marimbaphone, cymbal.

With *Trionfo di Afrodite*, Orff added a concluding work to his two scenic cantatas, *Carmina Burana* and *Catulli Carmina*. Poems by Catullus and Sappho, together with a chorus from Euripides' *Philoctetes* have been arranged to portray an Antique wedding celebration. Greek and Latin texts are thus unified, the elements joining perfectly and indistinguishably in that Catullus and Sappho themselves represent a unity. Catullus took the Greek lyric as a model, in order to revive its world in a Roman form.

The settings here are essentially different from those of the 'ludi scaenici' of *Catulli Carmina*. There, Catullus's poems were not set as verse, but given a new rhythm with a new dramatic effect. In *Afrodite*, however, the settings preserve the verse rhythms, while supplying a particular intensity of stylisation.

The inevitable comparison between *Afrodite* and Stravinsky's *Les Noces* can only be concerned with superficialities. *Afrodite* is something quite other than the mere transference of Stravinsky's supposed model to a context of Mediterranean antiquity. Moreover, it is not just 'a display of the composer's remarkable creative power, approaching preciosity.' (Moser) *Afrodite* is the immediate, ecstatic representation of the mystery of the Antique, pagan world.

The work is concerned with the 'epiphany of Afrodite'. It forms, significantly, with *Carmina Burana* and *Catulli Carmina*, a tryptich, to be performed together under the title of *Trionfi*. It is not concerned to represent a mythological figure—in this case Venus, Fortuna, Afrodite—as in the Renaissance ceremonial processions from which the idea of *Trionfo* is derived. Rather, developing the deeper implications, it 'unfolds dramatically a new, elemental experience and understanding of the divine and wordly powers of love, in different places, times and stages.' (Schade-waldt) *Carmina Burana*, *Catulli Carmina* and *Trionfo di Afrodite* provide three great linked illustrations of the world-theatre's view of the Western spiritual tradition in its different stages and places. It spans 2,500 years, from medieval to early Greek times. 'It travels back along the road by which we climbed from our own beginnings.' (Schadewaldt) *Trionfo di Afrodite*, with the actual appearance of the Goddess of Love herself, brings the tryptich to its climax. She associates herself with the wedding, which is 'the cosmic transfiguration of love in a cultic ceremony essential to the continuance of society. It reflects the divine cosmic processes in the mystery of union. But we must experience the whole tripartite structure of this manifestation of love: the elemental lived experience (*Carmina Burana*), the fateful demoniac power (*Catulli Carmina*), and the holy cosmic ordering (*Trionfo di Afrodite*). Until, as in Euripides, there is the climax of the epiphany of the Goddess as Queen of the World, the Triumph of Aphrodite.' (Schadewaldt)

Apollonian and Dionysian spiritual attitudes are sounded together in an astonishing way. Orff himself has become Grecian. He shows here, too, his familiar complexity of psychological approach in a combination of pious seriousness and solemnity with the 'Attic salt' of Aristophanic irony and mockery ('Lied vom Bettschatz', 'Exercete juventam!'). As with 'Cour d' Amours', the character of these episodes is well indicated by the interpretative markings on the score.

Technically, *Trionfo di Afrodite* is marked by the most extreme stylisation. This stylisation does nothing to weaken the elemental power of the music. The score is further notable for its most thorough exploitation of the expressive power of pure melody. All statement is immediately and directly concentrated in the singing voice. The point has been discussed earlier in some detail.

The orchestra plays a merely supporting role; it is never the main bearer of expression. The accompaniment often consists solely of tremoli chords at the octave. Its vocabulary is amazingly similar to that of Debussy's *Martyre de St. Sebastien*, a work with which *Trionfo di Afrodite* is connected also in the expression of a pagan spirituality. In contrast to *Catulli Carmina*, *Astutuli* and *Antigonae*, *Trionfo di Afrodite* re-introduces the full orchestra with strings, though naturally the percussion is still highly important.

I. 'Wechselgesang der Jungfrauen und Jünglinge an den Abendstern, während man auf Braut und Bräutigam wartet' (Catullus). (Alternate song to the evening star for maidens and youths, while awaiting the bride and groom.) Glissandi, extended melismas and choral recitations, characteristic diminished seconds, typify this alternate chorus with soprano and tenor soli. It rises to the bold, wide-ranging choral melisma of the finale.

II. 'Hochzeitszug und Ankunft von Braut und Bräutigam' (Sappho). (Wedding procession and arrival of bride and groom.) This is a two-part chorus, with sopranos set against bass voices. The music becomes increasingly breathless and urgent up to the climax of 'Cheoire!'.

III. 'Braut und Bräutigam' (Sappho). (Bride and groom.) This derives entirely from the sound of the Greek text. The melody, highly stylised, with its leaping intervals, melisma and chromaticism, becomes directly and solely the vehicle of expression. There is a clear connection with the Tiresias scene of *Antigonae*. Though the music conveys a mood of ecstasy, its restraint is such that it never rises above forte, and eventually subsides to pianissimo. The final 'Eis aei' is a Western, Christian, rather than a Greek, form of expression.

IV. 'Anrufung des Hymenaios und Preislied auf Hymenaios' (Catullus). (Invocation and song of praise to Hymenaios.) The first chorus surges forward in a great wave. The tonality characteristically alternates between C major and D major, in a way which recalls Stravinsky's *Petroushka*, though the device is one which Orff generally favours. Here is a full artistic development of what is merely sketched in *Catulli Carmina*. The song of praise is built on a single-bar ostinato. Everything is formed and expressed in terms of declamation, with rhythmic dislocation an important element. A ground-bass serves to establish tonality.

V. 'Hochzeitliche Spiele und Gesänge vor dem Brautgemach' (Catullus). (Games and songs outside the bridal chamber.) The first part, in which the bride is summoned to the bridal chamber, is in clear succession to *Catulli Carmina*. The song refers back to an episode in the earlier work. In 'Die Braut wird zur Hochzeitskammer geleitet' (the bride is led to the bridal chamber) the rhymically spoken word comes into its own. After the ecstatic 'Io Hymen', comes the mocking of the bride-groom's best friend, a recitation against a percussion background which provides the true 'Attic salt' mentioned earlier. The direction on the score, 'gesticolando assai, esagerando con teatralita', is the key to the psychology of the scene. The chorus greets the speech of their leader with laughter and jeering, before finally breaking out again into the ecstatic refrain. The leader of the chorus invites the bride and the groom to enter the bridal chamber in a passage of declamation similar in style to *Antigonae*. A middle section, 'Sed abit dies', is sung in an octave—fifth cadence. After the lyrical chorus 'Eher wird einer Afrikas Sand und die funkelnden Sterne zählen' (One could sooner count the sands of Africa and the glittering stars) there is the finale 'exercete juventam', shouted 'provocante' by the chorus and leader.

VI. 'Gesang der Jungvermählten in der Hochzeitskammer' (Sappho). (Song of the newly-weds in the bridal chamber.) This is an ecstatic duet. The pair speak to each other entirely in Greek

verse (see also III). This scene, together with 'Braut und Bräutigam', is one of the most important examples of Orff's use of
pure melody as the basis of expression, and is undoubtedly the
climax of its ecstatic lyricism (examples 5 and 6).

Orff pointed out in connection with the 'Cour d'Amours'
section of *Carmina Burana* that the whole psychological content of
the music could be gathered from the titles and interpretative
markings. In 'Hochzeitsgemach' nearly every musical phrase has
such a marking: sempre molto rubato—ardente—dolce—
sospirato con abbandono—quasi un sospiro—più intenso—esul-
tante—affanato assai—sempre più infiammato—etc. Even the
shortest episode contains the widest range of psychological
variation. Here especially the close-knit form gives immediate
and ecstatic expression to the melody.

VII. 'Die Erscheinung der Afrodite' (Euripides). (The epiphany
of Aphrodite.) The great power of Eros is summoned in a final
chorus which exposes the secret heart of the mystery in all its
fullness. The work ends with the irrational noise of the orgiastic
screaming of the Chorus ('trasportato').

COMOEDIA DE CHRISTI RESURRECTIONE

Composed 1955. First performance: Württembergisches Staats-
theater, 21 April 1957. Musical director: Heinz Mende. Producer:
Wieland Wagner. Designer: Wieland Wagner. The Devil:
Ernst Ginsberg. First performance on Bavarian Television: 1956.
Producer: Gustav Rudolf Sellner. Musical director: Karl List.
Designer: Franz Mertz.

Orchestra: 3 grand pianos, 2 harps, 4 double basses, timpani,
xylophone, tenor xylophone, marimbaphone, 2 glocken-

spiels, tubular bells, triangle, antique cymbal, cymbals, tam-tam, bass drum.

In the *Osterspiel* and the *Weihnachtsspiel: Ludus de nato Infante mirificus*, which followed five years later, the main emphasis falls on Orff's own text. *Carmina Burana*, *Catulli Carmina* (apart from Orff's Latin framework), and *Trionfo di Afrodite* involved the dramatic arrangement of pre-existing texts. *Der Mond* followed the pattern of the fairy-tale; *Die Kluge* was a free treatment of a familiar theme. *Astutuli* and *Bernauerin*, however, are entirely Orff's own texts. Even the earlier works displayed Orff's characteristic use of language. In *Bernauerin*, the Monk's sermon, the witches' scene, the lyrical love scenes and the powerful last act all bear the mark of his individuality as a poet for whom Bavarian dialect is a means to a quite personal creative achievement.

What *Bernauerin* and *Astutuli* began, the two sacred plays bring to full maturity. Speech is dominant during the whole course of the action except at the beginning and the end, where the music surmounts it. Obviously this organisation is far from anything one might think of as operatic. Here, as well as in *Oedipus der Tyrann*, Orff's central concern is convincingly exposed: a revelation of language ('Sprachaufsch liessung') emanating from the spoken word and venturing in accordance with intensifying demands for expressiveness into the more distant realms of the specifically musical.

Wolfgang Schadewaldt in the programme for the first performance of the *Resurrectione* wrote: 'Today one realises more and more clearly that Orff's work, seen as a whole, is developing in accordance with a subconscious law towards a universal poetry. The quintessence of mankind—the mankind of the European spiritual scene, controlled mainly by the powers of love and fate —is embodied by a new musical dynamism in the voices of different peoples, the spirit of different ages and places: Greece, Rome, medieval Germany. The Easter play of the Resurrection of Our Lord is a new, essential creation of this European universal poetry of Orff's. It brings into the theatre a historically developed form, the form of the Easter play which, springing from the cultural climate of the early Middle Ages, soon took on the character of folk drama. The play deals with a crucial moment in world history: that moment when the Resurrection of Christ ushered in a new era. It is also a manifestation of cosmic powers; Evil, in the traditional shape of the Devil, tries to prevent the Resurrection of Our Lord, but is forced to succumb to the power of Heaven.

'This sacred event is, however, treated with reverential indirectness through the use of folk images. The Roman soldiers who guard Christ's tomb are Bavarians, rough fellows who soon turn to dicing and card play. The Passion of Our Lord is mirrored in the meditative attitude of a few quieter, more sympathetic soldiers. The Devil, disgustingly unkempt, is also watching over the tomb, and he is more and more drawn towards the soldiers' game. But 'der Preller wird geprellt,' (the biter is bitten) as the choir in Orff's 'little world-theatre' of *Der Mond* said. The Devil—basically the stupid Devil of fairy story and legend— while enjoying his triumph over the soldiers, loses the main prize. Jesus has risen. The 'trionfo' of heavenly power is implicit in the downfall of the Devil, who, even if he can still cast his evil shadow over the world, must do so now with his dignity impaired; for, while the heavenly choirs sing in jubilation, he, in a blind rage, chops off his tail with an axe.'

This simultaneous contrast of the Angels' rejoicing in the resurrection, and the fury of the Devil is one of the poetic climaxes of the work. Orff's dramatic power is evident within the compass of a few bars. Accompanied by 'Christ ist erstanden,

Hallelujah!' and 'Totus Mundus jubilat, resurgit cum deliciis', the
Devil shouts, 'An Strick, a Schlingen, a Leitern, a Gift, a Messer,
a Beil, dass i mir selber an Schwanz abhacken kann!' (a rope, a
halter, a ladder, poison, a knife, an axe so that I can chop my tail
off).

Another outstanding scene is that of the Devil's conjuration at
the tomb where, the moonlight glinting on his amulet, he recites
his magical incantations. These consist of scraps of Latin and
German, forming in their sound pattern a melody of speech. The
purpose of the conjuration is to summon the fiends and demons
to the task of confining Christ to the tomb: 'dass er nit mehr
aufstehn kann! Adhuc, adhuc, adhuc: Larvae, Lemures, Maen-
ades, Manes, Incubi, Succubi, omnes Daemones! Includite, con-
cludite, praecludite, occludite, observate, obsignate hoc sepulcri
saxum: So stoss i den Riegel für!' The continuation of the spell
is also an occasion to go back to the use of old formulae of exor-
cism: 'Ausblasn des Licht und im bodn vergrabn. Die Finstern
hat's packt, hat's gfressen, aufgfressen, die gibt's nimmer her!'
(Blow out the light and bury it. Darkness has grabbed it, eaten it,
swallowed it and will never give it back).

Music dominates the structure only at the beginning and the
end. The Prooemium (Nenia ad sepulcrum canenda) opens with a
'Chorus mulierum lugentium' (altos), an introductory lament of
Greek women for Adonis, which is an interplay of Christian and
Pagan elements wholly characteristic of Orff. It continues with
the Chorus Angelorum (boys' voices), Vox mundana (soprano
solo) and Vox luctuosa (bass solo). A free instrumental cadenza
introduces this section, which, after a series of climaxes, finally
subsides again to a repetition of the Adonis lament sung on a
pedal D, with the instrumental accompaniment only at the
octave. The dark, full sound of the Greek ὂ ὀτοτὂ' establishes
the tone-colour of the lament.

The main, spoken scene at the tomb follows and this ends with the Cantus 'Christ ist erstanden', out of which grows the concluding musical section. The German song of jubilation is set against the oldest Greek song of resurrection, the song of the anchorites (basses). Finally, to this is added a Latin song of rejoicing in the reawakening earth: 'O fortunate anima'. This brief final chorus of the work ends with a melismatic 'Jubilus'.

Where a complete performance of the *Weihnachts* and *Osterspiel* is to be given on the same evening, the *Osterspiel* comes second though it is the first in order of composition. In the same way, the composition of *Antigonae* preceded that of *Oedipus*.

LATER CHORAL WORKS

Some new choral works composed in the fifties are the stylistic precursors of *Osterspiel*. The collection of a cappella choral settings, *Concento di Voci*, 1954 opens with the *Tria Catulli Carmina, Sirmio (Catulli Carmina II)*, written in 1931 and subsequently revised. The second collection of poems by Catullus in Latin for mixed choir a cappella, like the first, was inspired by an earlier visit to the home of the poet, to Lake Garda and the Sirmio peninsula.

Sirmio comprises a sequence of three poems: (1) 'Jam ver egelidos', (2) 'Multas per gentes', (3) 'Sirmio'. The composition is made up of loose, latinised faux-bourdon settings. At the same time, it throws into relief the palpable dynamic force residing in urgent recitation. Contrasts between solo and tutti are the main feature of the second and the third pieces, where the ecstatic, conductus-like declamation of three high voices above a pedal bass has as its climax the rapturous 'Ah' of the full choir.

The second part of *Concenti di Voci*, 1954, is the revised version of a choral setting from *Schulwerk*, Volume V: *Laudes creaturarum, quas fecit Beatus Franciscus ad Laudem et Honorem Dei*, for eight-part mixed choir (in the original language). First performance: Solingen, 21 July 1957. This poem is St. Francis's famous song to the sun. The whole work is a single unbroken arc in a mixture-style on a bourdon foundation. Orff's performance of the work on the piano has left a lasting impression. The 'Laudes' really sounded out in accordance with his marking: 'Estatico, sempre molto rubato'. The vitality and repetitiveness of the 'Eis aiona-Chor' of *Catulli Carmina* are transformed into an expression of ecstatic religious feeling. The increasingly intense recitation of the leading three-voice *organum* section offers no relaxation. The breathless praising of God subsides only partially to a single-tone psalmody to make way for the powerful ending. The 'Molto ecstatico' finale of the work, 'Laudate e benedicete lu mi Signore e rengratiate e servite a Lui', ends with two strongly accented Amens.

The third part of *Concenti di Voci* is *Sunt lacrimae rerum, Cantiones seriae*, for six-part male voice choir with tenor, baritone and bass solos, to texts from Orlando di Lasso and Ecclesiastices III. The work was written in 1956 and is dedicated to the town of Solingen, where it was first performed on 21 July 1957. The score is marked: 'The important matter of the division and distribution of voices is left to the discretion of the chorus master, and will therefore always vary according to the given circumstances. The printed score is merely an indication of the intended sound-character of the music.' When one recalls that Orff was strongly stimulated by Renaissance music, one may see in these instructions a reflection in a work of his own of the freedom which Renaissance composers allowed to their interpreters.

As in *Sirmio*, the three poems, sung without a break, are organised into a dramatic unity. The first chorus is a lament on the transitory nature of the world: 'Omnia deliciarum et pomparum saeculi brevi finis'. The second poem is on the text: 'Omnia tempus habent et suis spatiis transeunt universo sub coelo' (Ecclesiastices III, verses 1-8). This ends with an Orffian 'Estalto'—a crying out for peace, in complete contrast to Orlando di Lasso's setting, which ends 'in pace'. The third section, for baritone solo, 'erompente e molto pesante', takes up questioningly the last line of the previous chorus: 'Et tempus pacis?' (compare the final conversation of the shepherds about peace in *Weihnachtsspiel*). Then Orff introduces his own text: 'Eripe nos, Domine, ex ungulis mordacibus horribilis istius daemonicae . . .' (Drag us, O Lord, from the deadly claws of the fearful devil called Dejection, Sadness, Melancholy. Be cheerful, friends, and full of trust). The work ends with a tenor solo, 'Dammi il paradiso', which recalls 'Dormi ancora' from *Catulli Carmina*.

All three sections have the simplest sound pattern, clearly displaying the 'Klangrezitation' in mixture writing, and make lively use of solo-tutti contrasts, in which the choral groups pass from one to the other, in the manner of a hocket, the words: 'mors, dolor, luctus, pavor'. The first chorus is marked 'con gran tristessa', the second, 'sibillino' and the third, 'erompente e molto pesante'. The solo recitation of the text, 'the fearful devil', and the brief injunction, 'Be happy', is followed by the broader 'Dammi il paradiso' for choir with tenor solo.

In 1955/1956 Orff composed the Schiller choruses, *Die Sänger der Vorwelt* and *Nänie und Dithyrambe*.

Die Sänger der Vorwelt, elegiac hymn for mixed choir and orchestra. Composed 1955 to a commission from Deutscher Sänger-Bund for the XIV Deutscher Sänger-Bund Festival 1956 in Stuttgart. First performance Stuttgart, 3 August 1956, by Philharmonischer Chor under Fritz Mende.

Orchestra: 2 pianos, double bass, harp, percussion.

The text: 'Sagt, wo sind die Vortrefflichen hin, wo find ich die Sänger, die mit dem lebenden Wort horchende Völker entzückt?' (Tell me, where have the splendid ones gone; where can I find the singers who have given delight to the listening peoples with the living word), is given a musical form which might be described as choral drapery. The vocal recitation of the 'allegro pesante' to a certain extent runs parallel to the ecstatic 'Sonnengesang des Heiligen Franziskus'. But the melodic line is more wide-ranging and more soaring, the whole character more tremendous, with a full-bodied piano accompaniment underlying the choir. The dominant features are recitations on one note or at the octave, and choral recitations with the character of fauxbourdons. Urgent, clashing instrumental rhythms drive the work to its climax on a course which is full of contrasts. As far as the interpretation of the text is concerned, the climax is reached in the pianissimo ending on the word 'kaum' in 'Denn noch von aussen erschien, im Leben, die himmlische Gottheit, die der Neuere *kaum* noch im Herzen vernimmt.' (Still from without there appeared in life the heavenly Deity, which the newcomer *hardly* perceives in his heart). In this single word the whole meaning of the poem is concentrated. In its repetitiveness, it is the probe with which Orff explores this meaning to the roots. We will find similar procedures in the other two Schiller choruses. They demonstrate the individuality and variety of Orff's revelation of language (Sprachaufschliessung).

Nänie und Dithyrambe for mixed choir and orchestra. Composed 1956. Dedicated to the Philharmonische Gesellschaft Bremen. First performance: Philharmonische Gesellschaft Bremen, 4 December 1956, under Hellmut Schnackenburg.

Orchestra: 8 flutes (piccolos), 4 pianos (8 players), 2 harps, percussion (glockenspiel, xylophone, tenor xylophone, one or

10

more marimbaphones if available, castanets, tambourine, antique cymbal, cymbals, tam-tam, bass drum).

Nänie und Dithyrambe form a unity with sharply contrasting elements. In his small scale works for chorus, as in his full-scale stage works, Orff is concerned to realise the full dramatic and visual potentialities as well as those of gesture. In both media he drives towards ever sharper contrasts achieved by the simplest means. Each of his works derives its individual character from the nature of the particular text. The revelation of language (Sprachaufschliessung) is a basic element in Orff's style and mode of expression.

In the lament of *Nänie:* 'Auch das Schöne muss sterben' (Beauty must also die), all the music emanates from the sound of the words. At the beginning there is a rhythmic single-note recitative, which, arising wholly from the text, is recitative and aria in one. This simple example demonstrates the identity of music and language. Schiller's text is set by Orff in the following way:

EXAMPLE 16
(Nänie, first 9 bars)

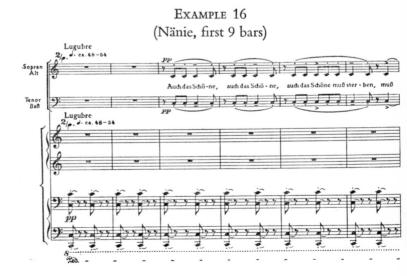

The whole piece is built on this text, and its rhythm, which is in no way an ostinato as has often been imagined, is maintained throughout. The rhythm is in itself the most important factor in conveying the meaning of the words.

From the 'Lugubre' opening, with its unison recitation for mixed choir, the work rises in its central section to an exciting climax, which brings into play the full instrumental resources. The culmination is reached at a great choral melisma on the words: 'Siehe, da weinen die Götter' (Look, the Gods are weeping). From this point, the work returns to the spirit of the opening, again revealing through music the full meaning of Schiller's words.

Dithyrambe is the ecstatic counterpart to *Nänie*. The punctuation of powerful piano chords on a percussion base mark the scansion of the text, which is brought out in the unison of the chorus. The work is in strophic form. The repeated units are given an instrumental accompaniment of ever-increasing force, forming an unbroken line and moving towards a finale in which the ecstasy drives beyond the rational sense of the Schiller poem to the irrationality of pure sound. Groups of Greek syllables (Euan, euan, euai, euai), which are not part of Schiller's text, dominate 'molto estatico' this irrational section. In its ecstatic outburst the music overwhelms the text. Orff's free setting penetrates Schiller's poem to its depths.

LUDUS DE NATO INFANTE MIRIFICUS:
EIN WEIHNACHTSSPIEL

Composed 1960. First performance: Württembergisches Staatstheater Stuttgart, 11 December 1961. Musical director: Heinz Mende. Producer: Paul Hager. Designer: Leni Bauer-Ecsy. The Witch: Mila Kopp.

Orchestra: Orchestra in concealed pit: piano, 2 timpani, tenor xylophone (chromatic), bass xylophone, musical glasses, steinspiel, guiro, angklung, 3 wood blocks, slit drum, rattle, bamboo sticks, ratchet, brush, 2 cymbals, 2 cymbals with bass drums, 2 bongos, large tom-tom, 3 kongas, large tam-tam, 2 tam-tams (2 different-sized tam-tams are fitted one inside the other, leaving a hollow space. This space is filled with small pebbles and the sound is produced by gyrating the instrument. See note to Page 35 of score).

Behind the stage: wind-machine, thunder sheet.

Orchestra and choir behind stage, pre-recorded on tape: 2 pianos, 2 harps, celesta, 3 double basses, organon, kettle drums, bass drum, glockenspiel, metallophone, xylophone, marimbaphone (2 players), bass xylophone, 3 triangles, cymbal, 2 pairs of small cymbals, 2 antique cymbals. Choir of Angels (sopranos and altos), Voices of Sleeping Flowers (very high-pitched children's speaking voices), Voice of Mother Earth (deep alto).

Like the *Osterspiel*, *Weihnachtsspiel* has its roots in the medieval mystery play and in its folkloristic developments (particularly in the addition of comic and allegorical episodes). It too stands as one of Orff's great poetic achievements, the music stemming basically from the language. The text is once again in the homely Bavarian dialect, with its pithy turn of phrase, against which is set the Latin of the Church. Mother Earth interjects a short phrase in Greek.

In *Osterspiel*, the rebirth of Nature is associated with the resurrection of Christ as a single act of salvation, which is seen, without sectarianism, as a cosmic event in the battle between the power of God and the Angels, and the demoniac powers of the Underworld. In *Weihnachtsspiel*, the birth of Christ is seen in the context of the same cosmic struggle. The work, drawing its life from the most intense cosmic tensions, truly belongs to the 'world-theatre'. While in *Osterspiel* Christ and his resurrection are opposed by the Devil himself, in *Weihnachtsspiel* it is the entire infernal world of the witches which seeks to frustrate the birth. 'The Witches' mime is the dramatisation of a desperate defensive struggle . . . The fear of the Son of Man which possesses 'die Obern, die Grossn' of *Osterspiel* attacks the Witches in *Weihnachtsspiel* when they think of the time of the Child's maturity. The threat of imminent defeat inspires them to continue the struggle even when all seems to be lost.' (O. Oster) *Osterspiel* is seen therefore as the second part of the struggle between God and the Devil, which brings, in the Resurrection, the final victory for the forces of salvation. Also, in the *Weihnachtsspiel*, the Holy Family do not appear on the stage; they are not even mentioned by name, but are referred to as 'The Child', 'The Woman', and 'The Man'. Bethlehem is, however, named. The brightness of the sacred event is reflected both in action and in narrative, particularly in the Shepherds' vision.

In the first scene we find the Witches in a cave, watching in a magic mirror the Woman and the Man on their way to Bethlehem, and trying to crush them with magic storms. This scene of conjuration develops into great climaxes such as 'Wind und Weh', with its onomatopoeic Latin interjections, rich in pictorial images, ending vividly with: 'Lasst's Schneewinder treibn, werft's di Windschaufeln auf! Windrader, Treibwinder, hellischer Blasbalg, Blasbalg vom Teifl! Schicks Gfrier, gross-machtinge Gfrier! Hauts Gfriernägl nei, dass allsamt verbeint, verbeint und versteint!—Menda Sibilla, so zwing' ma den Stern . . . so zwing' ma den Zauber, den Spruch und den Stern!' (Let snow-storms hurl, shovel up the wind, wind wheels, driving winds, hellish bellows, bellows of the Devil. Send frost, terrible frost sharp as nails, so everything is bone-hard, bone-hard, stone-hard. Menda, Sibilla compel the star, compel the magic, the spell and the star.) The Witches, thinking themselves victorious, end the scene with diabolical laughter.

In the following scene, the Shepherds, who have sheltered from the snow-storm in the cave, tell us how they rescued the straying couple from a snow pit. Two of the shepherds have a dream-vision in which they see the events at Bethlehem interwoven with the journey of the three Kings and the overshadowing vision of the Pietà. As a poet, Orff creates pictures worthy of the Golden Legend. One must mention also the profundity and robustness of language in the discussion of the text, 'Pax hominibus'. The shepherd who is overwhelmed by the vision is challenged by a sceptic; 'Itzt glangst ma, Kreizteifi! Itzt hab i schon gnua von dein dappertn Traam! Vom pax habn-s gsunga und von de hominibus? Dass i net lach!! Wie magst na an solchernen Schmarrn no verzahln? An pax, an pax bei de hominibus? So deppat ko do koar Engl net sein, dass er sowas daherredt!' (I've had enough, the Devil take it; I've had enough of your daft dream. They sang about pax and hominibus, did they? Don't make me laugh! How

can you talk such rubbish? Pax, pax to hominibus? No Angel
could be so stupid as to tell you such nonsense.) The shepherds
go to see the miracle in Bethlehem, leaving behind the sceptic to
look after the sheep.

In the last scene, the moon glistens over the snow-covered
landscape. Children appear, carrying candles, while distant music
sounds from on high. Voices of Angels sing: 'Plaudite, canite,
sonite . . . puer est natus in Betlehem'; the Children sing: 'Eia o
res miranda'; the Voices of the Flowers, who are being wakened
from their sleep under the snow by the light of salvation—the
Spring of Mankind—sing: 'Primula, primula, primula veris!
Crocus, Auricula, auri auriculae, audi, audite, aures erigite, aures
auriculae, hört ihr das Licht?' The text of the Flowers particularly
demonstrates Orff's extreme sensitivity to verbal music, by
which he can expose depths of meaning beyond the level of
rational sense, to be apprehended only in the sound phenomenon
of the language itself.

Everything strives towards Resurrection. The cosmic spiritual
event casts its light over the entire universe. The universal happi-
ness spreading from the Resurrection is, however, qualified by
Mother Earth's 'ouk estin hora' (The hour is not yet come).

The Witches appear again in a fury about their setback. The
old Chief Witch is given lines which show once again Orff's
poetic depths: 'Wart's ab, wart's ab, des Kindl im Stall, des kimmt
uns net aus. Lassts es no gross werdn! Mit'm Schnee, mit'm Wind
und mit'm Wettergspiel richt' si da nix! Des muss ma anderst,
viel anderst anlegn. D'Menschn, d'Menscherleit, die müssts
verführn, die san leicht anfällig, des warn die von eh. In d'Menschn müssts fahrn, die müssts hinterführn, müssts willfahrig
machn; müssts ihna schön tun, Schmeichwörter gebn; und san
s'amal handsam, müssts Bosheit einpflanzn, Narrheit und Blind-
tum! Die Menscherleit, die, die bringn, wanns sein muss, an jedn

ans Kreiz!' (Wait, wait, the child in the stable will not escape us. Just let it grow up. The snow, the wind and the weather won't do us any good. We must make quite a different plan. Men, mankind, we must lead astray. They have always been shaky. We must attack them, deceive them, make them obey us. Flirt with them, flatter them, and once they are softened up you must plant wickedness, stupidity and blindness. Then Man will bring to the Cross whoever he is told to.)

The Witches disappear. Once again the Voices of Angels sound in the heavens, and the Children sing their 'Eia o res miranda— Wir bringen das Licht; wir bringen den Schein, wir suchen den Schlüssel fürs himmlische Tor!' (Eia o res miranda—we bring the light, we bring the gleam, we search for the keys to the gates of heaven.) 'Laudate Dominum', which ends all medieval mystery plays, ends this work also.

The structure of the music at the end of *Osterspiel* and *Weihnachtsspiel* has a similar pattern. However, in *Osterspiel* the Lament serves only as an introduction whereas in *Weihnachtsspiel* the music of the Witches' recitation with its percussion base, extends into the first scene of the action. The Shepherds' scene in *Weihnachtsspiel*, which is purely unaccompanied spoken dialogue is analogous with the scene 'Vor dem Grabe' in *Osterspiel*. The demoniac Witches' music, the Christmas music, to which the Latin text adds a ritualistic note, and which, incidentally, is a 'music from on high', and the 'Voices of the Flowers' are, though extremes, nevertheless musically connected. For the first time, two radically contrasting worlds of sound confront each other. The first scene, which is given to the demoniac world, is dominated by the percussion orchestra in the orchestral pit. In the last scene, the angelic music from on high, which is recorded on tape, is set against the Voices of the Flowers and the voice of Mother Earth, which are also recorded. The singing of the children in the snow is live. The range of the music stretches from the highest children's voices to the deepest woman's voice of the Earth Mother.

The Witches' orchestra, which is obviously a development from *Bernauerin*, presents a powerful al-fresco block of percussion music. For the first time, Orff uses guiro, konga, angklung and the pebble-filled tam-tams, which intensify the hardness and sharpness of the sound. The Witches recite rhythmically to the percussion, the modulation of their voices being sharply differentiated. This wild demoniac scene has incredible brio and a most exciting intensity of expression. The storm-spell, 'Wind und Weh', with its waves of glissandi and the sound of the guiro may be cited as a particularly clear illustration. In all its ecstasy of demonism, all its fury, the tone-colour here has a quite individul shade of the most subtle variability.

Against the infernal clatter of the percussion music, the heaven-music stands in symbolic contrast. Here, the more delicate instruments, generally in the higher registers, come into their own: harps, celesta, the electric organ 'organon' (which is also important in *Oedipus*), glockenspiel, metallophone, marimba-phone, triangle, cymbal, etc. This bright music of an ornamental character comes down to us from on high with a truly heavenly sound.

OEDIPUS DER TYRANN
Ein Trauerspiel des Sophokles von Friedrich Hölderlin

Composed 1957/58. Dedication: Summo Atque Amplissimo Ordini Philosophorum Universitatis Literarum Eberhardo Caro-linae Tubingensis Hoc Opus Dedicavit Carolus Orff Monacensis Doctor Philosophiae Honoris Causa Tubingensis Anno MXMLIX. First performance: Württembergisches Staatstheater

Stuttgart, 11 December 1959, as part of an Orff Week. Musical director: Ferdinand Leitner. Producer: Günther Rennert. Designer: Caspar Neher. Oedipus: Gerhard Stolze. Jokasta: Astrid Varnay. Tiresias: Fritz Wunderlich. Kreon: Karl Bauer.

Orchestra: 6 Grand pianos (1-4 also with two players), 4 harps, mandolin, celesta, glass harp, 9 double basses, 6 flutes (also piccolos and 2 alto flutes), 6 oboes, 6 trombones, organon, 5-6 timpani, percussion (12-18 players): steinspiel, 2 xylophones, marimbaphone, 5-6 tenor xylophones, 2 bass xylophones, 5 wood blocks in different sizes, large wood clapper, 2 bongos, 2 timbals, large tom-tom, 3 kongas, 2 bass drums, 3 tambourines, castanets, triangle, sistrums, 3 pairs cymbals, 3 cymbals, antique cymbals, tubular bells, 3 glockenspiels (the 3rd with keys), metallophone, 3-5 tam-tams in different sizes, 2 Javanese gongs.

Behind the stage: 8 trumpets, several large tam-tams, to be struck with cymbals.

Since the first performance of *Bernauerin* in 1947, the Stuttgart theatre has provided Orff's art with an excellent home. The Intendant, Dr. W. E. Schäfer wrote in the programme for the first performance of *Weihnachtsspiel* in 1960: 'It may be said without exaggeration that Orff, the Bavarian, has found in our city an artistic home; it is the landlord, not the tenant who should be grateful.' After *Bernauerin*, the first German performances of *Trionfi* (1953), *Osterspiel* (1957), *Weihnachtsspiel* (1960) all took place in Stuttgart. For the re-opening of the bombed Kleines Haus in the 1963/64 season, the first performance of Orff's latest version of *A Midsummer Night's Dream* was given. *Oedipus* is dedicated to the Philosophy faculty of the Württembergische Landes-Universität Tübingen in gratitude for the honorary doctorate bestowed on Orff on the occasion of his sixtieth birthday. The Orff Week, of which the first performance was part, provided a unique opportunity for hearing Orff's major works together and as a whole. Wieland-Wagner's production of *Antigonae* Günther Rennert's production of *Der Mond*, with sets by Leni Bauer-Ecsy, and Paul Hager's production of *Trionfi* with J. P. Ponelle as designer, were all performed. The *Schiller Choruses* were given under Heinz Mende at a matinée, during which Orff himself read *Astutuli*.

Shortly after the Stuttgart performance, *Oedipus* was produced in Munster and Nuremberg, thereby demonstrating that, given the proper direction, even small companies could be equal to the demands of the work. The memorable performances at the Bavarian State Opera, Munich (23rd May 1961, Musical director: Joseph Keilberth. Producer: Heinz Arnold. Designer: Helmut Jürgens.) and the Vienna State Opera (27 April 1961, under Heinrich Hollreiser. Producer: Günther Rennert. Designer: Caspar Neher) followed. Contrary to *Antigonae*, which gained ground very slowly at first but then with steadily increasing momentum, as performances in Italian and Croatian testify, *Oedipus* has made rapid progress.

Orff's style always demands a new and individual kind of interpreter, but in the two Greek tragedies this demand is at its most insistent. A number of prominent artists have mastered the style perfectly. The unforgettable performances of Hermann Uhde and Carlos Alexander as Kreon in *Antigonae*, the greatness of Gerhard Stolze's portrayal of Oedipus, Christl Goltz's Antigonae and Jokasta, Astrid Varnay's Jokasta, Josef Traxel's Tiresias, Martha Mödl, Fritz Wunderlich and many others are noteworthy. At the same time, one must not forget the choruses, who have the greatest part to play in the tragedies.

Oedipus and *Antigonae* are closely related works; they retain the same relation to each other in Orff's setting as they have in the original. Sophocles wrote *Oedipus* a long time after *Antigonae*. As far as we know, *Antigonae* was first performed in 442 B.C.

and *Oedipus* 15 years later. This interval encompassed a considerable change of style. The case is similar with Orff; ten years separate the two works.

The essential dramatic differences between them have been pointed out by Hölderlin in his 'Anmerkungen zu *Oedipus* und zur *Antigonae*', where he briefly indicates the structure of the tragedies. The tragic climax of *Oedipus* comes at the end, in the second part. In *Antigonae*, it comes in the first part and what follows is merely the consequence of the tragic events in the first part. In both works the Tiresias scenes represent a dividing line and a kind of emotional regulator. In *Oedipus* the scene shores up the first part against the dramatic force of the second; in *Antigonae*, it is the second part which has to be protected from the high drama of the beginning. This regulating function places Tiresias in the second act of *Oedipus* but in the fourth of *Antigonae*.

Orff's *Oedipus* looks back to *Antigonae*, not vice versa, and the musical relation between the two works has to be considered in this light. Orff began his setting of *Oedipus* with a style developed through many years, and with the experience of a great number of performances of *Antigonae* behind him. Drafts of five complete versions of the first scene (Priest-Kreon) exist. A comparison of these indicates the methods by which Orff worked out a style specific to a setting of *Oedipus*. A fair copy of the first version occupies 100 pages; the final version has 28.

When one considers that *Oedipus* has 1492 lines to the 1310 lines of *Antigonae*, one realises that the music must be concise in the extreme. In place of a broad musical setting, the work called for a specifically Orffian style of speech and declamation. In contrast to *Antigonae*, with its generally sung or psalmodic tone and few spoken lines, *Oedipus* in the main embodies the sound of language in pure speech and recitation, using a more wide-ranging musical setting to bring to each crucial point of the drama, whether majestic or horrifying, the sharpest possible emphasis.

Oedipus comprises a variety of modes of speech. It is impossible to describe these with absolute precision; gramophone records and tapes are indispensible aids.

In *Oedipus,* Orff uses:

(1) speaking voice with only rhythm indicated (Kreon's entry, No. 20 in score, or Oedipus, No. 51, etc.).

(2) free spoken word on a musical base (Tiresias scene, No. 65 ff., and the great choral lament which ends the third act). Here solo voices from the chorus speak the intensely significant words against a rhythmic background.

(3) melodrama, which is a special form of the free spoken word (life story of Oedipus, No. 160). Here only certain words are given a tonal accompaniment—a partial musical base.

(4) and finally, something quite special, a speech-aria (Kreon, No. 118 ff.), quasi cantando on a rhythmic ground. The words are treated melodically rather than rationally.

The contrasts both between the different speech modes and between singing and speech which Orff draws within the narrowest compass form an important characteristic of this style of speech and declamation. While Jokasta in her speech seems to have a feminine single-mindedness (No. 146 ff.), Oedipus speaks freely and without restraint (No. 160 ff.). The chorus is at first (No. 134) in rhythmic speech and later (No. 136) is sung.

The change is quite abrupt when the emphasis on certain words or the accentuation of their meaning demands it. Thus (No. 45) the chorus breaks from pure recitation of the address to Jupiter into the sung call, 'Vater'. Example 17 shows a parallel, though less abrupt effect from Jokasta's 'Ein Spruch kam von Lajos' (No. 146 ff.).

It must also be remembered that the full register of vocal inflexion is available in each of the modes of declamation—the rhythmic choral declamation at the ghastly appearance of the blinded Oedipus (Nos. 266-269) ranges from a shocked scream to a horrified whisper. Thus one may understand how richly expressive this juxtaposition of speech and singing can be, both in large architectonic structures and the smallest single instances. The characteristic spoken-sung melody, which is at the same time a revelation of language and of psychology, justifies, because of the many forms it takes, some further examples. Oedipus's speech (No. 215) is particularly instructive. Here the confident, spirited vocal line to the text: 'Ich aber will als Sohn des Glüks mich haltend, des wohlbegabten, nicht verunehrt werden . . . Und so erzeugt, will ich nicht ausgehn so' ('so' is on a held high A) suddenly breaks off and: 'dass ich nicht ganz, wess ich bin, aus-forschte,' is spoken suddenly, without accompaniment. (I shall remain the child of Fortune, the richly endowed; I shall not be dishonoured . . . With such a parentage, I will not rest until I

EXAMPLE 17

learn exactly who I am.) With that, Oedipus goes out. These few
spoken words ('libero' and at the end 'molto stentato') open up
a whole psychological world.

Oedipus's account of his life (No. 168) provides another illustration. 'Bin ich bös? Bin ich nicht ganz unrein? und wenn ich fliehen muss, darf auf der Flucht die meinen ich nicht sehn, noch gehn zur Heimath; oder soll ich seyn zusammen mit der Mutter, gejocht zur Hochzeit, soll ich den Vater morden, Polybos, der mich gezeuget und mich aufgenährt?' (Am I wicked? Am I not utterly impure? Must I go into banishment, not seeing my people, not returning to my home? Shall I be forced into marrying my mother and murdering my father, Polybos, who begot and reared me?) is sung, but what follows is an unaccompanied spoken interjection, 'sfrenato': 'Würd' einer, der von unser einem urtheilt, die Sache nicht von rohem Geist' erklären?' (Would not anyone who judged our case see behind it some brutal spirit?) Then Oedipus breaks out 'molto appassionato', accompanied by crashing fortissimo chords on the pianos, high-pitched flute and oboe trills and high-pitched marimbaphone and tenor xylophone tremolos: 'Nein, nicht, o du der Götter heilig Licht, mag diesen Tag ich sehen, sondern lieber schwind' ich von Menschen, eh ich sehe, wie solch ein Schimpf des Zufalls mir begegnet!' (No! Never, O sacred light of the Gods shall I see that day. Rather will I leave the world of men than meet such an infamous fate.).

One curious passage, in which Oedipus interprets Kreon's oracle, serves as our final example: 'Denn alles werd' ich thun, entweder glüklich erscheinen mit dem Gotte wir oder stürzen.' (I will do all I can. We must either live happily with our Gods, or fall.)

No madrigalist would ever have made the vocal line leap upwards at the word 'fall'. The psychological explanation is that Oedipus does not believe that he will fall; he is completely sure of himself. The high G is sung falsetto and piano. Thus everything serves to make every last word yield its full meaning, everything serves the working out of the tragedy (Ex. 18).

EXAMPLE 18

The instrumentation of *Antigonae* arose out of a similar demand. While, however, in that score, Orff was exploring the problems of forming an appropriate body of sound, in *Oedipus*, the instrumentation is more in the nature of primary data. The first half of *Antigonae* is built entirely on piano and percussion, and the flutes, trumpets, etc., enter successively later. The instrumentation is another indication that if the two works are to be performed as a cycle, *Oedipus* must come after *Antigonae*.

The instrumentation of *Oedipus* is much more extended and varied than that of *Antigonae*. To the trumpets are added six trombones, enlarged percussion section as well as various drums, large clappers, bongo, timbal, large tom-tom, konga, celesta, glass harp, and an electric organ (organon). This latter instrument provided an unlimited range of sonorities, doubling the wind instruments, pure organ tone, mixture tone, and a kind of percussive staccato. It reminds one of Monteverdi's organo di legni and of the regal. In the Tiresias scene, where it combines with pianos, harp, steinspiel, xylophone, and glass harp, with a quite unreal vibrancy, it introduces us to an exciting new tone-colour (Nos. 65-68 ff.).

11

In the big choral lament (No. 179) the organon in a low register stands in contrast to high-pitched flutes and oboes; elsewhere (Nos. 251, 161 ff.) it is used in the manner of Monteverdi as an organo di legni.

The climax of the work comes at the entry of the blinded Oedipus, when eight trumpets, pre-recorded on tape, blare out through loud-speakers placed all round the hall to give a stereophonic effect. Oedipus appears to have served as his own priest in blinding himself as an act of sacrifice, the fulfilment of his mission. The horror is beyond good and evil. The trumpet call, in pure fifths, is not a lament or a howl, but a confirmation of the inexorable 'fulfilment', expressed with unsurpassable urgency. Then Oedipus breaks into endless human lamentation. The C, which with its fifth now sounds out, is the basic note of the whole work.

It is here that the style of the work can be seen most clearly. The parallel scene in *Antigonae* is her walk to the tomb. In both cases, the expressive forms, gesture and dance are of such clarity that they exclude naturalism and psychologising.

In comparison to *Antigonae*, the score of *Oedipus* shows a wider range of sound effects apart from the instrumentation. The trombone chords accompanying the chorus after the Tiresias scene (No. 98), and the mirror chord as Jokasta goes to sacrifice at the temple of the Demons (No. 188) provide clear examples. They are to be understood as sound symbols (Ex. 19).

The chorus (No. 218) with its effect of static sound makes a symbolic reference in a similar way. W. Keller has called such effects, 'Personanzklänge'. Winfried Zillig in *Variationen über neue Musik*, offers a more detailed explanation. Following an examination of the tonally inexplicable passages of *Trionfo di Afrodite*, he writes: 'In *Oedipus*, Orff makes a clear stride forward along this path. One cannot go far in this extraordinary score

EXAMPLE 19

without coming upon the chord C-E-G-B♭-D♭-E♭, which contains the tension of the diminished octave, and would theoretically be describable in terms of tonal music as a discord on the dominant of F minor, if, in the melodic minor, E in the ascending scale and E♭ in the descending scale came together. As it stands, however, one cannot fix its tonality; C major and G flat major emerge together. It consists of the first six notes of a twelve-tone row, made up of four thirds, of which two are major and two of the corresponding minor, standing in a tritone relationship. At the entry of the prophet Tiresias, there is a particularly daring chord: E♭-F-B♭-C-F-G♭-C♯-D, and in different instruments, C-D♭-F♯-G.

'As the singing voice adds to this a virtuoso melismatic orna-
mentation on the notes G♭, A♭, and B♭♭, a complex of ten
tones is arrived at, lacking only E and B for a complete twelve-
tone structure. Or, G major and D♭ major sound simultaneously, and in the next chord, F♯ major and G minor.
The first chord is in the same relationship as C major-G♭ major.
The second chord soon returns independently and unites C major
with D♭ minor, these two keys having the same third, E, or F♭.
In Jokasta's song at the beginning of the fourth act, one en-
counters a chord which seems quite baffling: F-A♭-C-D♭,
and above that, C♯-D-F♯-A. This is inexplicable tonally, but
it is clear enough if one realises that it is a mirror-chord with
D♭, or C♯, as the central note, from which the ascending
and descending intervals are the same. (See example 19.) One may
say that in *Oedipus* the sounds which do not yield a tonal explanation predominate, but, at the same time, the score is a miracle
of concentration. All harmonic effects are to be related finally to
the central tone, C with its dominant G and the dominant of the
modulation, D.'

Oedipus is built up with an economy characteristic of Orff, and
an admirable clarity of architectonic structure. With harsh and
even brutal force, Orff drives to the ultimate climax, 'Die
Sprache der Sprache zur Sprache zu bringen'. After the opening
dramatic scenes, the first powerful, ecstatic number in the score
is the chorus, 'O du von Zeus hold redendes Wort' (O, you
gracious oracle of Zeus), with its massive orchestral introduction.
The most notable features of the second act are the urgent,
rhythmical introduction, Oedipus's speech, 'Forschen will ich' (I
will seek), the magnificent Tiresias scene—with the same urgency
as, but otherwise so different from the equivalent scene in *Antigonae*—and the final chorus. In the third act occur the spoken
discussion between Oedipus and Kreon, with its hard percussion

base, Kreon's speech-aria, followed by the big Oedipus-Jokasta scene with chorus, in which Oedipus gives his account of his life, and the powerful choral lament, with its stressed melodic character on a pointed rhythmical ground. The fourth act begins with Jokasta's walk to the temple. The conversation with the messenger from Corinth, which starts hopefully, ends in deep tragedy. After the expressive, 'O Armer, wüsstest nie du, wer du bist' (O, poor man; if only you never need learn who you are), Jokasta goes out, uttering a death-foreboding shriek. The climax of the scene, which clarifies all that has gone before, comes at the chorus and the mounting excitement of Oedipus's conversation with the Shepherds. After his wild outburst, Oedipus goes out quietly. The fifth act is introduced by the messenger's report. It rises to the shattering climax of the appearance of the blinded Oedipus and the horrified scream of the Chorus. This is followed by the lament of Oedipus, which, filled with melismatic cries of pain, leads into the scene with Kreon, Antigonae, and Ismene. Here, the music recalls that of the walk to the tomb in *Antigonae*, and thus serves as a connecting link between *Oedipus* and its sequel. After a 'schwerem und langem Schweigen', there follows the final section of the work, which includes the last chorus: '. . . preist glücklich keinen, eh denn er an des Lebens Ziel gedrungen, Elend nicht erfahren!' (Call no-one happy until he has reached life's goal without misfortune).

DAS SCHULWERK

MUSIK FÜR KINDER

THE importance of *Schulwerk* in the corpus of Orff's work has been duly recognised. Orff achieved immediacy and vitality in his pedagogical as well as his theatrical work. Both spheres of his creative activity derive from a single root.

Orff withdrew the first version of *Schulwerk*, which was completed in 1935 after ten years' work at the Güntherschule. This version was arranged in a large number of separate booklets: rhythmic-melodic exercises, elementary piano and violin pieces, pieces for dancing and play. The subsequent five volumes of *Musik für Kinder* constituted the core of Orff's educational work. They were warmly received and have already been translated into several languages. *Schulwerk* is truly fundamental to the establishment of a technique of musical education for the present day. It was published between 1950 and 1954, under the editorship of Carl Orff and Gunild Keetman.

The immediate stimulus to revise the work came from the Bayrischer Rundfunk, whose Schools' section, under Annemarie Schambeck, proposed a series of programmes on Orff's *Schulwerk*. This plan was carried out between 1948 and 1952 by Gunild Keetman and Rudolf Kirmeyer under Orff's personal supervision, the music being performed by children. These broadcasts provided the basis and preparatory work for the new version.

From this time, the manufacturers produced in increasing numbers the new instruments, xylophones, glockenspiels, etc., which Orff called for. Today they have been generally adopted but, unfortunately, are known for the most part, by the name of Orff-instruments.

In the introduction to the fifth volume of *Musik für Kinder*, which appeared at Easter 1955, Orff confessed, 'The experience of nearly thirty years has gone into this work. Nevertheless, as an experiment, this first fundamental scheme is necessarily fragmentary. Much could only be indicated, and a mass of material had to be omitted entirely, to avoid undue fragmentation.'

What Orff implies by the title 'for Children' has already been suggested. Even the great demands of the last volumes can be met by the innate musical sense of childhood. The gradual development of technique is incidental. The method embodied in *Schulwerk* has been fully expounded in Wilhelm Keller's *Einführung*, which was published by Schott in 1954, together with Fritz Reusch's *Grundlagen und Ziele des Orff-Schulwerks*. As we have already discussed the theoretical aspects of the work in the first part of the book, all we need do now is to indicate its basic technique and structure.

The work is designed to awaken the imaginative musical powers of the child and to develop them in a way which the child will find enjoyable. The principal method is by improvisation. The first awakening of interest gives rise to elementary creativeness. Every exercise, particularly in the early stages, has the purpose of releasing this will to create out of the child's own discovery of his musical abilities. Rhythmic-melodic exercises, to equip the pupil for improvisation, together with speech exercises, form the foundation of the course. What is produced at this stage is not essentially different from the artistically more advanced treatment of the material, which constitutes *Urgrund* music in Orff's sense of the term. Even the speech exercises of the first volume demonstrate clearly 'the basic connection between the magic of word and sound and the physical movements of dance and gesture.' (W. Thomas)

The first volume introduces the pentatonic scale, beginning with two-note melodies. It goes down to the very first awakenings of music in the child. The volume supplies basic training in rhythmic-melodic exercises for voice and instruments, and the simplest forms are cultivated. The child is shown the primary material of music, free from conditioning. The literary material consists of rhymes and play-songs and there are many exercises on the texts, offering possibilities for improvisation. Naturally, there are also pieces written specifically for Orff's instruments.

The second volume introduces major tonalities, at first in bourdons of six and seven notes, and then in intervals showing the relation between the sounds of the first and second notes of the scale as well as the first and sixth. The classical function of harmony is ignored; the interest is in the direct experience of the sound. Indeed, although many of the examples are complex in sound, they are, in effect, experienced monophonically.

The third volume, with the introduction of the dominant in the major, considers form in terms of the functional cadence. The use of the dominant is set in specific opposition to the bourdons of the second volume, without, however, entirely excluding the latter. 'The exercises on the dominant lead into familiar musical spheres and, in conjunction with the previous exercises, help to develop a sense of style while avoiding the merely conventional, especially in improvisation.' (Introduction) Here he also treats the sub-dominant, and includes the intervals of the seventh and the ninth.

The fourth volume demonstrates the minor, together with the Aeolian, Dorian and Phrygian modes. These are treated in bourdons as well as in intervals, all of which are dealt with. Here the child is introduced to a new world. 'The texts are chosen to document an extensive experience of Nature and the human spirit. The childish note has, by now, been almost entirely superseded. The closest connections with the traditional folk-song are established.' (Introduction)

The fifth and final volume deals with the dominant in the minor, the fifth, with and without the leading note, and the fourth. The highest demands are made upon the pupil, particularly in the concluding section which includes such small masterpieces as *Sonnenhymnus des heiligen Franziskus*, *Jubilationes* and three pieces from *Wunderhorn*. The final part of the book, the second group of rhythmic-melodic exercises, with its speech-pieces and recitatives (three pieces from Goethe's *Faust*, a chorus from Sophocles, *An einem österlichen Tag*, *Quem queritis in sepulchro?*) lead directly to Orff's 'music of language.' The notes to these pieces provide important clues to Orff's speech and recitative forms. The entire work ends with the following four lines from the 'Walpurgisnachttraum' of Goethe's *Faust:*

> Wolkenzug und Nebelflor
> Erhellen sich von oben.
> Luft im Laub und Wind im Rohr,
> Und alles ist zerstoben.

A truly Orffian inspiration.

The spiritual significance of *Schulwerk* is as the key to the fundamentals of music. But the systematic instruction it provides leads, at the same time, from the primary basis of innate musicality to the world of historical musical forms, in exactly the same way as the concern with basic sound leads to an understanding of, and competence in tonality and the historical sound systems. The interest in bourdon, faux-bourdon, descant, etc., makes the pupil aware of the range of possible forms that a mechanical technique may command. The basic forms employed in improvisation are preparatory to the more complex forms of Western music.

Creative improvisation, in song and variation, canon, chaconne and rondo, develops naturally into the composition of more artistically developed kinds of music.

Apart from a consideration of the purely musical aspects of *Schulwerk*, the literary value of the texts must be stressed. Thomas ranks it with Herder's *Stimmen der Völker* and *Des Knaben Wunderhorn*. 'A wealth of European folk-culture is vigorously and effectively introduced.' Orff is most sensitively aware of sagas, fairy-stories, folk and children's songs, riddles and old saws as primal emotive material. In the first volumes examples of this literature are taken only from the German provincial dialects. It is mainly in the fourth volume that the choice of material extends to survey the whole Western folk tradition. European folk-song—German, French, Spanish, Italian and Scandinavian— are placed side by side with Old German and medieval Latin texts, and a wealth of ballad material from *Wunderhorn*. Although only a 'sketch', *Schulwerk* has from a literary point of view also, a rounded completeness. This quality, with the light it throws on music and language, and its value as a training in composition, makes *Schulwerk* an education to the Western inheritance.

Not only is the whole selection so organised that it brings into play the full range of spiritual refraction, the quintessence of the elemental as well as the Western, but each separate piece, as, on a larger scale are Orff's works for the theatre, is a revelation of childhood, of folk character, and a true revelation of Orff.

It is an easy and natural step from this wealth of folk culture to the pieces from *Faust* and the Greek chorus from Sophocles' *Antigonae*—easy and natural, thanks mainly to Orff's illumination of language, which breaks down all boundaries of time and nationality, and recognises only the oneness of living things. In the same way, we, to-day, justly place primitive art in a living relationship to the great Western masterpieces.

A glance through *Schulwerk*, and particularly the fourth and fifth volumes, reveals quite clearly that there is no basic difference in style or spiritual attitude between these pieces and the works for the theatre. Some pieces of the old (1935) collection have indeed found their way into the theatre. The 'Intrada' from *Bernauerin* and the melody, 'Trompeters, der in den Mond bläst' (*A Midsummer Night's Dream*) are derived from the violin exercises, and the children's song from *A Midsummer Night's Dream*, from the piano exercises. Further examples could be cited.

In July 1961 at the Academy for Music and the Arts in the Mozarteum in Salzburg, a centre and seminar for Orff's *Schulwerk* was established. Such a centre for teacher training and further research was necessary in view of the unforeseen way in which the practice of *Schulwerk* had spread throughout Europe in the last decade.

The many foreign language editions already published or in preparation bear testimony to this wide dissemination. English, American, Swedish, Flemish, French, Danish, Spanish, and Portuguese editions have already appeared. *Schulwerk* is being used also in Turkey, Italy, Yugoslavia, Greece, Israel, Finland, and Japan. Its effects are being felt with ever increasing strength.

It is of special significance for the work that Orff himself once again decided to set up a training centre with his long-standing collaborator, Gunild Keetman. As the theories of *Schulwerk* spread, the lack of specialist teachers became more and more apparent. The way was open for educational dilletantes, who ignored the fact that working with *Schulwerk* makes the highest demands on the teacher.

Orff also wished to avoid the one-sidedness of a purely musical education, and so, in accordance with the original scheme, training in movement is an important factor in the Salzburg course. Furthermore, the instruments for *Schulwerk* are being added to on lines suggested in earlier plans. All this was possible only under the auspices of an Academy which had as its Director and President a man like Dr. Eberhard Preussner, who has so thorough a knowledge of the ideas and methods of *Schulwerk*, and supports them so enthusiastically.

In an interview, Orff said: 'I never imagined that my educational efforts would win understanding and acceptance so quickly and so widely. When I was writing *Schulwerk*, I had merely the intention of providing my Bavarian homeland with a useful and practical course in elementary musical education. But these ideas have spread so much in the last ten years that now *Schulwerk* is being taught in over twenty languages. The 'Internationale Zentralstelle und Seminar für Orff-Schulwerk' was established in the Salzburg Mozarteum in order to provide a centre for these widely scattered efforts, a school and a home for *Schulwerk*, where it could be seen in practice, and also where exponents could meet for discussion and orientation. Apart from the two-year course for teachers who want to take a Diploma in *Schulwerk*, there are from time to time introductory and refresher courses.

'In addition to these training schemes, special research has been devoted to music therapy, and *Schulwerk* and its instruments are being widely used in nursing-homes, clinics, and in psychotherapy centres.'

JUGENDMUSIK

Apart from *Musik für Kinder*, *Schulwerk* also includes the subsidiary collection, *Jugendmusik*. It contains pieces taken mainly from the first version of *Schulwerk*.

Jugendmusik also includes *Weihnachtsgeschichte*, a play for children by Carl Orff, set to music by Gunild Keetman (1948.) This has been performed many times, both on the stage and on the concert platform. The new version of the 1929 *Cantus-firmus-Sätze* ('Ten old melodies for voice or instruments'), which appeared in 1954, was similarly incorporated. *Jugendmusik* also contains Orff's *Einzug und Reigen* (1952) and pieces respectively for recorders, for flute and drum, recorders and small percussion, and small percussion alone by Gunild Keetman. This collection is still being added to.

EPILOGUE

In this book we set ourselves the task of examining Orff's work in order to arrive at an understanding of its character. The individual nature of Orff's music has forced us to pay great attention to its spiritual background. His music cannot be understood in isolation from his theatre, nor his theatre without reference to the spiritual background which nourishes it, and out of which the world-theatre has sprung, to become the most significant new development in the present-day scene. The phenomenon of Orff shows itself in the 'spiritual exposition' which his work as a whole presents, and in the urge to elemental immediacy. He is significant not merely as a musician or as the creator of works for the theatre, but as a great chronicler of the culture and general spirit of our time, and as one who has given concentrated and profound expression to the 'zeitgeist' of our epoch.

The general nervous hurry of today, as reflected in most modern music, has no place in Orff's work, which rises and develops in large rhythms. Each work is born of an inner compulsion and matures slowly, like a natural growth. Seen as a whole, Orff's work has developed in quiet but irresistible rhythms to the point of its greatest intensity of radiation and effect. Orff was forty-two years old when *Carmina Burana* opened the way to world-wide success. After twenty years, the work has at last made its mark over continents. The war may have delayed the process, but, fundamentally, all Orff's work is subject to a slow rhythm of development. *Die Kluge*, similarly, did not meet with immediate success, though its popularity mounted with steadily increasing momentum. The *Entrata* took twenty-five years to establish itself. And even such a work as *Antigonae*, although acknowledged as one of the most original works of our time, is far from having reached the full height of its power and influence, not to mention *Oedipus der Tyrann*.

This image of a 'rhythm of development' is valid not only in Orff's case. One thinks of all the highly praised works which have enjoyed immediate success in the past, and are now no longer heard of.

It has already been mentioned that the writing of this book was subject to a condition that it should contain no purely biographical material. Orff's personality is, therefore, seen here only as it is reflected in his music. It is reserved for some other person at a later time to write a biographical study of Orff, an undertaking which would go far beyond the scope of this book and would call on the testimony of friends, pupils and collaborators from all periods of his life. Not least in importance would be Orff's extensive correspondence with his faithful publisher friends, Dr. Ludwig and Willy Strecker.

There would be much to say about his work with his pupils. From 1950 to 1960 Orff conducted a master-class in composition at the Munich Hochschule für Musik. We have not mentioned Orff's active collaboration in all important performances of his works, in the concert-hall, the theatre, on the radio, and in connection with his *Schulwerk;* here also his friends and colleagues would be called on to elucidate and delineate his life-story. A new and important task has fallen to him with the opening of the 'Zentralstelle und Seminar für Orff-Schulwerk' at the Mozarteum in Salzburg.

I have dealt here only with completed works. All the projects and plans which Orff failed to follow up—and if one knows his fiery and scintillating nature, one may be sure that there are many such—were placed outside my terms of reference.

Orff, looking back on all the work he has completed up to now, said of it, 'It is all primarily finger-exercises.' He thus indicated, with characteristic irony and understatement, that he has important plans for the future, which he mentions occasionally to his friends, but which, again, I was not allowed to refer to in this book.

Orff's remark to his publisher, in 1937, 'With *Carmina Burana* my collected works begin,' is further indication of the singleness of purpose which has marked his whole life's work. All his plans mature slowly. Whatever he composes in the future will be a thoughtful development from what he has composed up to now. It will evolve from a spiritual, idealistic centre, as have all his previous works.

APPENDICES

BIBLIOGRAPHY

(Selected)

Andreas Liess, Carl Orff—Idee und Werk, Atlantis-Vlg. Zurich 1955.

Carl Orff, ein Bericht in Wort und Bild, with contributions from E. W. Schäfer, K. H. Ruppel, G. R. Sellner, W. Thomas, B. Schott's Söhne, Mainz 2/1960; English edition 1961.

Ingeborg Kieckert, Die musikalische Form in den Werken C. Orffs, Bosse-Vlg. Regensburg 1957.

Udo Klement, Vom Wesen des Alten in den Bühnenwerken C. Orffs, (examination thesis) Leipzig 1958.

Curt Sachs and Oscar Lang, Einführung in die Neugestaltung von Orfeo, B. Schott's Söhne, Mainz 1925.

Wilhelm Twittenhoff, Orff-Schulwerk, Einführung in Grundlagen und Aufbau, B. Schott's Söhne, Mainz 1930.

Wilhelm Keller, Carl Orffs Antigonae, Versuch einer Einführung, B. Schott's Söhne, Mainz 1950.

Wilhelm Keller and Fritz Reusch, Einführung in 'Musik für Kinder' and Grundlagen und Ziele des Orff-Schulwerks, B. Schott's Söhne, Mainz 1954.

Wolfgang Schadewaldt, Carl Orff Trionfi, die Idee des Werks,

K. H. Ruppel, Trionfi, zur Geschichte ihrer Entstehung und Erneuerung durch C. Orff.

K. H. Ruppel, Carl Orff, Trionfi, Werk und Wirkung; Three contributions to the booklet issued by DGG, with their recording (German, English, French) 1957.

Ferdinand Etienne and Paul Vanderschaeghe, C. Orff, Handzame Uitgeverey Dewilde.

Helmut Klemnitz, Die Kluge von C. Orff; in: Die Oper, Schriftreihe zum Musikunterricht in der mittleren und höheren Schule, Berlin 1961.

Carl Niessen, Die deutsche Oper der Gegenwart, Bosse-Vlg. Regensburg 1944.

Otto Oster, C. Orff und das musikalische Theater, in Theateralmanach Desch, München 1947.

Erich Doflein, Das Musiktheater C. Orffs, in Musikalmanach Desch, München 1948.

Heinz Hackenbroich, C. Orff, in Musiker von heute; Pazeller-Vlg., Fulda 1949.

K. Laux, C. Orff, in Musik und Musiker der Gegenwart, Vlg. Spael, Essen 1949.

Walter Riezler, Neue Horizonte, Bemerkungen zu C. Orffs Antigonae, in: Gestalt und Gedanke, Jahrbuch der Bayr. Akad. der schönen Künste, Oldenburg, München 1951.

Erich Valentin, C. Orff, in Kleine Bilder grosser Meister, Bausteine für Musikerziehung und Musikpflege, B. Schott's Söhne Mainz 1951.

Günther Wille, Die Bedeutung der Musik im Leben der Römer, (Examination thesis) Tübingen 1951, page 250.

Hans Joachim Moser, Musikgeschichte in 100 Lebensbildern, Reclam-Vlg. 2/1958.

Wilhelm Zentner, Opernführer, Reclam 1953.

Karl H. Wörner, Neue Musik in der Entscheidung, B. Schott's Söhne Mainz 1954.

Wieland Wagner and W. E. Schäfer, Carl Orff zum 60. Geburtstage, Bayreuther Festspiele 1955.

Karl Michael Komma, Probleme der Hölderlin-Vertonung in Hölderlin-Jahrbuch IX/1955/56, Tübingen 1957, page 201 ff.

Siegfried Melchinger, Modernes Welttheater, Schünemann-Vlg. Bremen 1956.

Winfried Zillig, Variationem über neue Musik, Nymphenburger Vlgs-Buchhandlung, Munchen 1959.

Wolfgang Schneditz, Begegnung mit Zeitgenossen, Munchen 1959, pages 105-109.

Wolfgang Schadewaldt, C. Orff-Trionfi, Die Hölderlinsche Antigonae des Sophokles von C. Orff, Das Werk C. Orffs und sein neues Osterspiel, Zur Urauff. des Oedipus der Tyrann nach Hölderlin von C. Orff, in Hellas und Hesperien, Artemis-Vlg. Zurich 1960.

Andreas Liess, Carl Orff, in Encyclopédie de la musique, Ed. Fasquelle Paris 1961, volume III, pages 346-7.

Andreas Liess, Carl Orff in Collier's Encyclopedia, New York 1962.

Ernst Laaff, C. Orff, Musik in Geschichte und Gegenwart, volume X, pages 199-204.

Werner Thomas, Carl Orff in Riemann Musik-Lexikon XII edition, Schott Mainz 1961, volume II, pages 345-47.

O. E. Schilling, C. Orff, Neue Musikzeitung 1947.

K. H. Ruppel, C. Orff und das Theater, Musica 1948, Nos. 3/4, Kassel.

Ernst Laaff, Ein Revolutionär des musikalischen Theaters, Melos, Mainz 1949, No. 3.

Thr. Georgiades, Zur Antigonae-Interpretation von C. Orff, Österr-Musikzeitschrift, Wien 1949, No. 7.

Otto Oster, C. Orff, in Das Musikleben, Schott, Mainz, III 1950.

Otto Oster, C. Orff, Essay über einen Musikstil, Melos, Schott, Mainz 1950, No. 6.

Otto Oster, Unsere Musikfibel, Wesen und Bedeutung des Orff-Schulwerks, Musica, Bärenreiter-Vlg. Kassel, V 1951.

M. Christian Feiler, Das Orff-Schulwerk, in Das Musikleben, Mainz IV 1951.

M. Christian Feiler, Reform der Musikpädagogik: Das Orff-Schulwerk, in: Musik im Unterricht, Schott 1951.

Bruno Stäblein, Schöpferische Tonalität, zum Grossaufbau von Orffs Antigonae, Musica, Kassel 1952, No. 4.

E. Forneberg, Die Klage der Ariadne, Zwischen Monteverdi und Orff, in Musica, Kassel, 1952, No. 6.

K. Colberg, C. Orffs Wagnis, in: Neues Abendland, VIII/1953.

Heinz Zirnbauer, Die Quellen des Schulwerks, Zeitschrift für Musik, Schott 1955, No. 7.

Werner Thomas, Wortmagie und Klangmagie, in: Musik im Unterricht, Schott 1955.

Werner Thomas, Erklingende Sprache (Interpretationsversuch nach dem Schulwerk von C. Orff) in: Der deutsche Unterricht, Ernst Klett-Vlg., Stuttgart 1956.

Heinz Zirnbauer, Das Klassische im Werke C. Orffs, in Die pädagogische Provinz, Hirschgraben-Verlag, Frankfurt/Main 1960.

Helmut Schmitt-Garre, Neue Formen der Musikbühne, Schweizer Musikzeitschrift, 79/1939.

H. Rutz, C. Orff und sein Schulwerk, Rhythmisch-melodisches Spiel, Vorstufe der Persönlichkeitsbildung, In Österr. Musikzeitschrift VI/1951.

H. Staeps, Das Phänomen Orff oder: Magie und Manier, Österr. Musikzeitschrift VI/1951.

Everett Helm, Carl Orff, in The Musical Quarterly, Schirmer, New York, July 1955.

Roger Stengele, C. Orff et la musique moderne, in Revue générale Belge, April 1957.

Willibald Götze, C. Orff, in Streven, Amsterdam, Dezember 1958.

Guido L. Luzzatto, L'Antigonae di C. Orff, in: Dioniso, Bollettino dell'Istituto Nazionale del Dramma Antico, Siracusa, July-Oct. 1956.

Ignace de Sutter, C. Orff, in Jong Kulturleven/Belgien, 1958, Nos. 8/9.

Arnold Walter, C. Orff's Music for children, in The Instrumentalist, Evanston/Illinois, U.S.A.

E. Doflein, C. Orff und seine Bernauerin, Schweizer Musikzeitung 1958, III.

Wilhelm Keller, C. Orff, in Stilportraits der Neuen Musik, page 42 ff., Berlin 1961.

LIST OF MUSICAL EXAMPLES

List of Illustrations

INDEX OF ORFF'S WORKS

JUVENILIA

Lieder: *Eliland* (Stieler), *Märchen* (Haushofer), *Des Herzens Slüzzelin*, *Toskanische Volkslieder* (Heyse), *Der Tod und die Liebe* (Muenchhausen), others to texts by Uhland, Lenau, Hölderlin, Münchhausen, Baumbach, Storm, Lingg, Heine (*Die Wallfahrt nach Kevelaar*), Arndt, Nietzsche, the Eddas, etc.
Songs with Orchestra (Dehmel).

Instrumental and Choral Works:
Also sprach Zarathustra (Nietzsche) 1912.
Tanzende Faune, for Orchestra 1914.
Treibhauslieder (Maeterlinck) unfinished 1914.
Monna Vanna (Maeterlinck) Symphonic poem, unfinished 1914.
*Choral pieces, 2 string quartets.

Operas:
Gisei, das Opfer (after *Terakoya* by K. Florenz) 1913.
*Sketches for *Aglavaine et Sélysette*, *Der Tod des Tintagiles* (Maeterlinck), *Traumspiel* (Strindberg).
*Incidental music (Shakespeare, etc.).

EARLY WORKS

*Incidental music to *Leonce und Lena* (Büchner) 1918.
*Lieder to texts by Franz Werfel, Trakl, Klabund, Nietzsche, etc., around 1920.
Des Turmes Auferstehung, Cantata (Werfel) 1920.
Kleines Konzert for harpsichord and wind instruments (based on 16th Century lute pieces) 1927.
Entrata (after William Byrd) for five instrumental groups 1928. Arranged for small orchestra by Robert Wagner. First performance (1930) 1941.
Cantus-firmus-Sätze, (12) 10 old melodies for voice or instruments (1929) 1954 (see also *Jugendmusik*).
Cantatas to texts by Werfel (*Werkbuch I*) 1929:
Veni creator spiritus. First performance 1930.

Der gute Mensch. First performance 1930.
Fremde sind wir.
Cantatas to texts by Bert Brecht (*Werkbuch II*):
*Von der Freundlichkeit der Welt.
Vom Frühjahr, Öltank und vom Fliegen.
Catulli Carmina I, seven choral settings a cappella 1930 (see also
    Catulli Carmina, 'Ludi scaenici' 1943):
    'Odi et amo'
    'Vivamus, mea Lesbia'
    'Lugete, o Veneres'
    'Ille mihi par esse deo videtur'
    'Ammiana'
    'Miser Catulle'
    'Nulla potest mulier'
Catulli Carmina II, three choral settings a cappella 1931:
    'Jam ver egelidos'
    'Multas per gentes'
    'Sirmio' (see also 'Sirmio', *Tria Catulli Carmina*, in *Concento di voci*
    1954
*Realisation of the *St. Luke's Passion* (Bach?) etc. 1931.

MATURE WORKS

STAGE WORKS
Monteverdi realisations:
    Orpheus, freely adapted (D. Günther) (1925) 1940.
        Playing time 60 minutes. Piano score 3188.
    Tanz der Spröden, freely adapted (D. Günther) (1925) 1940.
        Playing time 30 minutes. Piano score 3186.
    Klage der Ariadne, freely adapted (Orff) (1925) 1940.
        Playing time 12 minutes. Piano score 2874.
    Lamenti, Trittico teatrale tratto da opere di Claudio Monteverdi
    (consisting of the three above works) 1958. Piano score 4768.

OTHER STAGE WORKS
    Carmina Burana 1935/36. First performance 1937. Playing time
    65 minutes. Miniature score 4425, piano score 2877. Edition for
    two pianos and percussion by W. Killmayer 4920.

Der Mond 1937/38. First performance (1939) 1947. Playing time 90 minutes. Piano score 3196.

Die Kluge 1941/42. First performance 1943. Playing time 90 minutes. Miniature score 4580, piano score 2868.

Catulli Carmina, Ludi scaenici 1943. First performance 1943. Playing time 45 minutes. Miniature score 4564, piano score 3990.

A Midsummer Night's Dream 1939. First performance (1939, 1944) 1952. Playing time, the whole evening. Piano score 3992.

Die Bernauerin 1944/45. First performance 1947. Playing time, the whole evening. Piano score 3997.

Astutuli 1945/46. First performance 1953. Playing time 50 minutes. Piano score 4314.

Antigonae (Hölderlin-Sophocles) 1947/48. First performance 1949. Playing time, the whole evening. Miniature score 5025. Piano score 4026.

Trionfo di Afrodite 1950/51. First performance 1953. Playing time 45 minutes. Miniature score 4566, piano score 4306.

Trionfi (consisting of *Carmina Burana*, *Catulli Carmina*, *Trionfo di Afrodite*). First performance 1953.

Commedia de Christi Resurrectione 1955. First performance 1956. Playing time 55 minutes. Piano score 4932.

Oedipus der Tyrann 1957/58. First performance 1959. Playing time, the whole evening. Piano score 4996.

Ludus de nato Infante mirificus 1960. First performance 1961. Playing time 60 minutes. Piano score in preparation.

CHORAL WORKS WITH INSTRUMENTS

Die Sänger der Vorwelt (Schiller) 1955. First performance 1956. Playing time 11 minutes. Score 4699, piano score 4367.

Nänie und Dithyrambe (Schiller) 1956. First performance 1956. Playing time 11 minutes. Score for piano (4 hands) and percussion 4939.

UNACCOMPANIED CHORAL WORKS

Concento di voci: Sirmio, Tria Catulli Carmina (1930).

                   Laudes creaturarum 1954. First perf. 1957.

                   Sunt lacrimae rerum 1956. First perf. 1957.

See: Cantus-firmus-Sätze (1929) 1954. Score 4454.
Vier Chore aus Catulli Carmina 1942.

ORFF–SCHULWERK (1930/35) 1950/54
Musik fur Kinder, 5 volumes. 3567/3568/4451/4452/4453.
Single editions: Reime und Spiellieder 3574.
          Frühling und Sommerbeginn 4893.
          Lieder fur die Schule, books I–III 5140/42.
Grundübungen (collected by E. Werdin) 4455.
Foreign editions:
American edition: Music for children. 4470/72 5135/36.
Teacher's Manual (Doreen Hall) 4898.
English edition, volumes I–IV 4865/68.
Swedish edition: Musik för barn, volumes I–II 4860/61.
Dutch edition, volumes I–II 4871/72.
Nederlandse Volksliederen (Marcel Andries) 4891.
French edition: Musique pour enfants.
Chansons originales françaises extraites de l'oeuvre complète,
          4473.
Chansons enfantines (Gunild Keetman) 4890.
Danish edition:
Danske Borne –og folkesange (Minna Lange-Ronefeld) 5147.
Portuguese edition: Musica para Crianças, part I in preparation.
Cancoes para as escolas 5145.

Jugendmusik
Carl Orff, Piano exercises 3561;
          Violin exercises I 3571;
          Violin exercises II 3572;
          Die Weihnachtsgeschichte (text) 1948, 3563;
          Einzug und Reigen, 1935, (1936) 1952, 3564;
          Cantus-firmus Sätze (1929) 1954, 4454.

All works are published by B. Schotts Söhne, Mainz. The early
lieder were published by E. Germann, München-Leipzig, but are no
longer in print. All works marked * are unpublished.

A DISCOGRAPHY

Compiled by Arthur Boyars

Monteverdi Realisation—Lamento d'Arianna
Elisabeth Höngen (contralto), F. Leitner and R. Reinhardt
(harpsichord) and A. Graeser (double-bass). Deutsche Grammophon APM 14020 (GB) and ARC-3005 (USA)

Carmina Burana—Scenic Cantata (1935–36)
Trötschel, Kuen, Braun, Hoppe, Bavarian Radio Chorus and
Orchestra conducted by Eugen Jochum. Deutsche Grammophon
LPM 18303 (GB & USA).
Giebel, Kuen, Cordes, West German Radio Chorus and Cologne
Radio Symphony Orchestra conducted by Wolfgang Sawallisch.
Columbia 33CX1480 (GB) & Angel 35415 (USA)
Harsanyi, Petrak, Presnell, Rutgers University Choir and Phila-
delphia Orchestra conducted by Eugene Ormandy. C.B.S.
BRG72169* (GB) & ML–5498* (USA)
Srubar, Subrtova, Tomanek, Czech Singers Chorus and Czech
Philharmonic Orchestra conducted by Vaclav Smetacek.
SUA10409 (GB) & Parliament 161* (USA)
Babikian, Hager, Gardner, Houston Corale and Houston Sym-
phony Orchestra conducted by Leopold Stokowski. Capitol
PAR–8470* (USA)
Stahlman, Ferrante, Meredith, Choir and Hartford Symphony
Orchestra conducted by Fritz Mahler. Vanguard 1007* (USA)

Entrata—After William Byrd—for Orchestra and Organ (1928,
revised 1940)
Vienna State Opera Orchestra conducted by Hermann Scherchen.
Westminster XWN 19013* (USA)

Der Mond—A Narration with Four Episodes (1937–38, revised 1941)
Christ, Schmitt-Walter, Graml, Kuen, Lagger, Peter, Hotter,
Rosner, Hollowaay, Philharmonia Chorus and Orchestra con-
ducted by Wolfgang Sawallisch. Columbia 33CX1534–5 (GB) &
Angel 3567* (2) (USA)
Excerpts: Columbia 33CX1815* (GB)

Die Kluge—The Story of the King and the Wise Woman (1941–42)
Cordes, Frick, Schwarzkopf, Wieter, Christ, Kusche, Kuen, Prey,

Neidlinger, Philharmonia Orchestra conducted by Wolfgang Sawallisch. Angel 3551(2) (USA)
Excerpts: Columbia 33CX1810* (GB)
Catulli Carmina—Ludi Scaenici (1930, revised 1943)
Kupper, Holm, Bavarian Radio Chorus, Four Pianos and Percussion conducted by Eugen Jochum. Deutsche Grammophon DGM18304 (GB), second record of Trionfi, Deutsche Grammophon 3–DGG 18483/5 (USA)
Roon, Loeffler, Kamper, Mrazek, Gielen and Klein (pianos) and percussion, Vienna Chamber Choir conducted by Heinrich Hollreiser. Vox PL8640 (GB & USA)
Die Bernauerin—Ein Bairisches Stück (1947)
Abridged Version: Gold, Liewehr, Holm, Fölser, Barthels, Delcroix, Fröhlich, Harsdorff, Kürzinger, Michal, Renar, Rösner, Schwaiger, Wisheu, Bavarian Radio Chorus and Orchestra conducted by Ferdinand Leitner. Deutsche Grammophon LPM 18408 (Germany)
Antigonae—Setting of Hölderlin's Version of Sophocles' Tragedy (1949)
Borkh, Hellmann, Stolze, Uhl, Häfliger, Borg, Plumacher, Engen, Bavarian Radio Chorus and Orchestra conducted by Ferdinand Leitner. Deutsche Grammophon 3–DGG 18717/9* (USA)
Trionfo di Afrodite—Concerto Scenico (1953)
Kupper, Lindermeier, Wiese-Lange, Holm, Delorko, Böhme, Bavarian Radio Chorus and Orchestra conducted by Eugen Jochum. Third record of Trionfi, Deutsche Grammophon 3–DGG 18483/5 (USA)
Music for Children (1930–34)
Volumes 1 & 2. Chorus of the Children's Opera Group, Chorus of Bancroft's School for Boys, Speech Ensemble from the Italia Conti School, with Instrumental Ensemble directed by Carl Orff, Gunild Keetman and Walter Jellinek. Columbia 33CX1549–50 (GB)
Volumes 5 & 6. Tölzer Boys' Choir, Cologne Children's Chorus, Munich Staatlichen Hochschule Musik Kammerchor, Instrumentalists directed by Carl Orff. Harmonia Mundi 2-Harmo. 30654/5 (Germany).
*Denotes availability in Stereo

INDEX OF NAMES